THE COMMONWEALTH AND INTERNATIONAL LIBRARY

Joint Chairmen of the Honorary Editorial Advisory Board

SIR ROBERT ROBINSON, O.M., F.R.S., LONDON

DEAN ATHELSTAN SPILHAUS, MINNESOTA

Publisher: ROBERT MAXWELL, M.C., M.P.

LIBERAL STUDIES DIVISION

General Editors: E. F. CANDLIN AND D. F. BRATCHELL

EARLY NINETEENTH CENTURY EUROPEAN SCIENTISTS

EARLY
NINETEENTH CENTURY
EUROPEAN SCIENTISTS

Edited by

R. C. OLBY

PERGAMON PRESS

OXFORD · LONDON · EDINBURGH · NEW YORK
TORONTO · SYDNEY · PARIS · BRAUNSCHWEIG

Pergamon Press Ltd., Headington Hill Hall, Oxford
4 & 5 Fitzroy Square, London W.1

Pergamon Press (Scotland) Ltd., 2 & 3 Teviot Place, Edinburgh 1

Pergamon Press Inc., 44–01 21st Street, Long Island City, New York 11101

Pergamon of Canada, Ltd., 6 Adelaide Street East, Toronto, Ontario

Pergamon Press (Aust.) Pty. Ltd., 20–22 Margaret Street,
Sydney, New South Wales

Pergamon Press S.A.R.L., 24 rue des Écoles, Paris 5e

Vieweg & Sohn GmbH, Burgplatz 1, Braunschweig

Printed in Great Britain by A. Wheaton & Co., Ltd., Exeter and London

CONTENTS

v

LIST OF PLATES

ACKNOWLEDGEMENTS

The Editor is grateful to the following for permission to reproduce plates and to make quotations:

Plates 1, 2, 3, 9, The Royal Institution.
      4, 5, 6, Heinemann.
      7, Trustees of the British Museum.
      10, 11, 12, Oxford University Press.
      15, Williams & Wilkins, Baltimore.

The quotation on p. 150 is reproduced from the *Dictionary of National Biography* by kind permission of the Oxford University Press.

INTRODUCTION

THE early nineteenth century saw exciting developments in many fields of science. Here five topics are reviewed in the context of seven biographies—chemistry under Humphry Davy and Berzelius, optics under Thomas Young, photography under Daguerre and Fox Talbot, geology under Lyell and statistics under Quetelet.

In this period Lavoisier's work was extended and corrected and the foundations of a quantitative system of chemistry were laid. Lavoisier had listed 33 elements in 1789, amongst which he included the alkali earths. The caustic alkalis, soda and potash, on the other hand, he excluded as he believed they would one day be shown to have a compound nature. Humphry Davy, with the aid of the voltaic pile, succeeded in breaking down the latter thus discovering sodium and potassium. In like manner also he isolated magnesium, calcium, strontium and barium from the alkali earths, magnesia, lime, strontia and baryta. He realized that the electric current generated by a voltaic pile was not produced, as Volta believed, merely by the contact of dissimilar metals, but is the *result* of a chemical reaction. And conversely the decomposition of an electrolyte when a current is passed through it is brought about by the passage of electricity. This led Davy to consider an electrical theory of chemical combination. The Swedish chemist, Berzelius, on the other hand, not only considered such a theory but developed and sophisticated it producing as a result his theory of dualism according to which all compounds consist of positively and negatively charged constituents, which may be single atoms or groups of atoms—the radicals.

Meanwhile the Quaker schoolmaster, John Dalton, provided a rational explanation for the recently established laws of constant composition and of multiple and reciprocal proportions. These observed regularities suggested the presence of discontinuities in matter, and Dalton regarded them as particulate in nature. His theory, first put forward in a lecture in 1803 but not published until 1807, was established by Berzelius on the basis of careful experiments and developed quantitatively so as to yield estimates for the relative weights of atoms. At the same time he put forward a logical system of chemical notation, which has survived to this day in a modified form.

While chemists were being asked to accept a particulate theory of matter, Thomas Young was trying to persuade physicists to accept a wave theory of light. The question as to whether light is best considered as a stream of particles or as a form of energy whose propagation is wave-like had been discussed before, but Young was the first to offer a serious challenge to the corpuscular theory. Henry Brougham's criticism of Young's work and Laplace's advocacy of the corpuscular theory did much to seal the fate of Young's attempt. Nevertheless he might have been successful had he regarded the waves as transverse and not longitudinal. Fresnel's parallel labours in this field, and his demonstration of the transverse nature of light waves undoubtedly played an important part in the ultimate establishment of the wave theory. Young's studies of Egyptology and physiological optics are also described in this volume.

The influence of light on silver nitrate had been reported in 1619; cameras in the form of camera obscuras had been in use since the fifteenth century at least; lenses of a sophisticated construction were widely used in telescopes and microscopes in the eighteenth century. But before the nineteenth century there was no known method for increasing the sensitivity of silver nitrate, or of developing and fixing the latent image. The process of discovering suitable agents was a lengthy one and was achieved by a long series of trial and error experiments. The obvious commercial value of success lent to these experiments an aura of secrecy and the inventors became involved in legal contracts, patents and law suits. The story of their struggle is told in the biographies of Daguerre and Fox Talbot.

Eighteenth-century geology was so dominated by Catastrophism—the attribution of the present structure of the earth to mighty catastrophies in the past—that the stratigraphy of Adam Smith and the uniformitarianism of James Hutton were largely ignored. Thus it came about that Charles Lyell was able to develop Smith's promising technique and Hutton's fruitful theory with momentous consequences for the science. The studies which Lyell and his friend, George Scrope, made of valleys and volcanoes yielded important evidence with which to attack the Wernerian geologists. Scrope's eye-witness account of the explosion which blew the last 800 ft off Mount Vesuvius in 1822 made clear the errors of the Wernerian view of volcanic craters as "craters of elevation". The greater part of the chapter on Lyell is devoted to his famous three-volume treatise, *The Principles of Geology*, volume one on the principle of uniformity, two on organic evolution and three on the structure of the earth's crust. But special attention has been paid to Lyell's views on evolution and to the extent of Darwin's debt to him.

In 1800 statistical techniques had already been used widely by politicians and by life insurance companies as an aid to achieving precision in forecasting a nation's needs and a man's life expectancy. In the hands of Laplace they found application in astronomy. Gauss applied statistics to field theory and arrived at an expression for the normal distribution of errors around the mean. But Quetelet was the first to show that deviations from the mean in the expression of biological characters are distributed through a population in accordance with Gauss's Law of Error. Quetelet also played a leading part in the organization of international conferences on statistics, thereby establishing links between the scattered band of statistical workers.

CHAPTER 1

SIR HUMPHRY DAVY, 1778–1829

DAVY was one of the few chemists who can be described as glamorous, and his dramatic rise from a country cottage to world fame and the presidency of the Royal Society has attracted many biographers. We shall therefore have relatively little to say about Davy's private life, and this chapter will be mainly concerned with his chemical researches, and in particular with his attitude to the atomic theory and his speculations concerning the nature of the chemical elements.

When Davy was born there on 17 December 1778, Penzance was a small country town in what was still the wild west, with smugglers and wreckers abounding. The town could boast at that time only one carpet; all the other houses had sand on the floor. Davy's father was a wood-carver, but he was frequently un-employed and at his death Davy's mother went into partnership with a French refugee and opened a milliner's shop. Davy's schooling was not at all what one would plan for a scientist; he began at Penzance Grammar School, where the master had a little rhyme that he repeated every time Davy was punished, which was often:

> Now, Master Davy,
> Now, sir! I shall have 'ee,
> No one shall save 'ee—
> Good Master Davy.

Not surprisingly, Davy did not show any signs of genius while at school, and he seems to have been rather idle and mischievous, with a reputation for being a good story-teller. Later in life he wrote to his mother: "After all, the way in which we are taught

PLATE 1. Humphry Davy.

Latin and Greek does not much influence the important structure of our minds. I consider it fortunate that I was left much to myself when a child, and put upon no particular plan of study, and that I enjoyed much idleness at Mr. Coryton's school. I perhaps owe to these circumstances the little talents that I have and their peculiar application."

But in 1795, when his father died, Davy decided that he must get down to work, and wrote out a formidable educational programme for himself. This included theology, geography, the sciences, logic, languages, rhetoric and oratory. At this stage he was apprenticed to an apothecary surgeon in Penzance, and began to make a few simple scientific experiments. Chemistry was becoming the most popular of the sciences; in Glasgow, Dr. Garnett attracted audiences of over 500 to his public lectures, and Dr. Beddoes in Oxford proved the most popular lecturer the University had known since the thirteenth century. In Paris, Fourcroy also attracted large and enthusiastic crowds, so the phenomenon was not confined to the British Isles. To us the surprising thing is how little was known in chemistry; Davy read two textbooks, one of them by Lavoisier, whose new chemistry was replacing the phlogiston theory, and the other by Nicholson, who edited an important scientific journal. This proved an adequate basis for Davy to begin research, and he performed original experiments on the nature of light and heat. He was at this time nineteen years old.

ON HEAT AND LIGHT

He followed Newton and most seventeenth-century scientists in supporting the kinetic theory of heat, that what we call heat is simply the rapid motion of the particles of which all matter is composed. In opposition to this, eighteenth-century workers had proposed that heat was a weightless fluid, which they called caloric. This theory explained readily why not all bodies conducted heat—it could not get through non-conductors—and the role of heat in chemical reactions. For on Lavoisier's view, heat

was a chemical substance which could combine with other substances, as happened during changes of state, from solid to liquid
for instance, when the heat absorbed became "latent", or combined. Caloric entered into chemical reactions generally, and
indeed appeared in Lavoisier's list of chemical elements. Davy
rubbed two pieces of ice together in a vacuum, and found that
they melted with the friction. This would have been inexplicable
to Lavoisier, for no heat fluid could have got to the ice; but on the
kinetic view there is no problem, for the rubbing would impart
more energy to the molecules of the ice, and cause it to melt.
Unfortunately, Davy's experiment was impossible; his air-pump
was home-made, and heat must have leaked in from elsewhere.
Credit for establishing experimentally that heat is a form of
energy belongs to Rumford, whose experiments were contemporary with Davy's, and to Joule in the next generation. None the
less, Davy's ideas were sufficiently interesting and suggestive to
excite the great Victorian physicist Lord Kelvin.

Although Davy considered heat to be a form of energy—his
language was different but that is what he meant—he believed
light to be a quite distinct phenomenon. Again following suggestions of Newton's, he considered light to be corpuscular and
therefore subject to gravitation. Light was for him a form of
matter, and he believed that its role in chemistry had been
grievously underestimated. Indeed, Davy sought to give to light
the position that caloric had held in Lavoisier's chemistry. He
wrote: "Oxygen gas (which the French nomenclators have assumed
to be oxygen combined with caloric) will be proved to be a substance compounded of light and oxygen. . . . The term phos-
oxygen . . . will I think be unexceptionable; it will express a
chemical combination of the simple substance light, with the simple
substance oxygen. . . ." When bodies burned, they united with the
oxygen, releasing the light that had been combined with it; we see
this light in flames. The role of light was not, according to Davy,
limited to inorganic chemistry: "Light enters into the composition
of living bodies. To understand the combinations is of infinite
importance to man. On the existence of this principle inorganic

compounds, perception, thought, and happiness appear to depend." Electricity might be, he believed, light in a condensed form.

These early views, published in 1799, were somewhat derided, and Davy withdrew them: "Facts have occurred to me", he declared in 1800, "with regard to the decomposition of bodies, which I have supposed to contain light, without any luminous appearance. Till I have satisfactorily explained these facts by new experiments, I beg to be considered a sceptic with regard to my own particular theory of the combinations of light, and theories of light in general." He vowed to avoid excessive theorizing in future; but fortunately his speculative genius was by no means muzzled, and later his hypotheses were just as exciting. He retained a secret belief in the importance of light—especially when combined with oxygen—throughout his life. But most of the theories that he formed so readily he was very ready to abandon or amend if they failed to fit the facts.

DAVY'S WORK IN BRISTOL

Davy's papers on heat and light were published by Dr. Beddoes, who had been Reader in Chemistry at Oxford but had been ejected for his well-founded but violent criticisms of the Bodleian Library, and for his enthusiastic support of the French Revolution. He had set up at Hotwells, near Bristol, a "pneumatic institution", to try to cure the sick by making them breathe various gases. And in 1799 he invited Davy to break off his apprenticeship and come to Bristol and join in the work and research at this institution.

Beddoes had married a sister of Maria Edgeworth, the novelist, and the Beddoes' home seems to have been a centre for literary men. There Davy met and became friends with Coleridge and with Southey, whose *Thalaba* Davy later saw through the press. Both Coleridge and Southey thought highly of Davy's own poetic abilities, but to modern taste his verse seems rather heavy and prosy. But Coleridge later went to Davy's lectures, he said, to improve his stock of metaphors.

PLATE 2. The properties of laughing gas being demonstrated at the Royal Institution.

Davy's greatest discovery while at Bristol was that nitrous oxide, which had previously been suspected of poisonous properties, was respirable, and indeed very pleasurably so. The gas appeared to have many of the advantages of alcohol without leaving a hangover, and breathing the gas soon became a craze. Davy published a book on the chemistry of the gas, and on its physiological properties, containing accounts of its respiration written by himself and various of his friends. He proposed that the gas be used in minor operations as an anaesthetic—as "laughing gas" it is still so used in dentistry—but no surgeons took up the suggestion, and patients had to wait about half a century before anaesthetics were adopted. But Davy wrote what have been described as some of the best subjective accounts of anaesthesia ever recorded.

Thus, on breathing nitrous oxide from a bag, he reported that "A thrilling, extending from the chest to the extremities, was almost immediately produced. I felt a sense of tangible extension highly pleasurable in every limb; my visible impressions were magnified, I heard distinctly every sound in the room, and was perfectly aware of my situation. By degrees, as the pleasurable sensations increased, I lost all connection with external things; trains of visible images rapidly passed through my mind, and were connected with words in such a manner, as to produce perceptions perfectly novel. I existed in a world of newly connected and newly modified ideas: I theorized, I imagined that I made discoveries. When I was awakened from this semi-delirious trance by Dr. Kinglake, who took the bag from my mouth, indignation and pride were the first feelings produced by the sight of the persons about me. My emotions were enthusiastic and sublime, and for a minute I walked round the room perfectly regardless of what was said to me. As I recovered my former state of mind I felt an inclination to communicate the discoveries I had made during the experiment. I endeavoured to recall the ideas: they were feeble and indistinct; one collection of terms however presented itself; and with a most intense belief and prophetic manner, I exclaimed to Dr. Kinglake, 'Nothing exists but thoughts! The universe is composed of impressions, ideas, pleasures and pains!' "

Davy did not follow up these experiments, for in 1800 Volta announced the discovery of the electric battery, which was a pile of zinc and silver plates in water, with some dissolved salt. This, in Davy's words, "was as an alarm bell to experimenters in every part of Europe; and it served no less for demonstrating new properties in electricity, and for establishing the laws of this science, than as an instrument of discovery in other branches of knowledge, exhibiting relations between subjects before apparently without connection, and serving as a bond of unity between chemical and physical philosophy." This was much less obvious than it is now in the first five or six years of the century, when the facts of electrochemistry were by no means established. It is to Davy that the credit must be given for the systematic application of the battery in chemical analysis, and for the attempt to link physics and chemistry by an electrical theory of the chemical bond.

Shortly after the appearance of Volta's original paper, Nicholson and Carlisle used a battery to decompose water into oxygen and hydrogen. In 1800 Davy published a series of articles describing his experiments with Beddoes' battery of 110 pairs of plates. He found that when water is electrolysed, rather less oxygen than one would suppose is given off; but this he explained by the solubility of oxygen in water. He found that with pure water between its plates, the battery would not work. This observation led him to suggest that the working of the battery depended on the oxidation of the zinc plates. "It appears", he declared, ". . . that the galvanic pile of Volta acts only when the conducting substance between the plates is capable of oxidating the zinc; and that in proportion as a greater quantity of oxygen enters its combination with the zinc in a given time, so in proportion is the power of the pile to decompose water, and to give the shock greater. It seems therefore reasonable to conclude, though with our present quantity of facts we are unable to explain the exact mode of operation, that the oxidation of the zinc in the pile, and the chemical changes connected with it are *somehow* the cause of the electrical effects it produces." This "chemical" theory, that the energy of a chemical reaction may be manifested as electricity, now seems the obvious one; but Volta, working forty years before the conservation of energy had been established, had suggested that the electricity was produced simply by the contact of dissimilar metals. On this view, a battery might produce electricity indefinitely.

Davy verified his chemical theory by using acids in the battery instead of water, for with an acid one would expect that the chemical action would be greater and therefore so would the quantity of electricity produced. And indeed he found that concentrated nitric acid was the most effective medium, so effective that Davy had to throw the pile into water to prevent its destruction, and got a shock in so doing. At about this time too he made a battery consisting of two fluids with a metal between them, instead of the more usual arrangement of two metal poles dipping into a fluid. This kind of battery would have been hard to account for on Volta's theory; but if one adopts the chemical theory then its explanation is no different from that of the ordinary battery. Davy also used his battery to boil water, by immersing a wire carrying a current in it, and to produce an electric arc.

Later he reported on this last experiment in a lecture; he began by producing sparks between metal terminals, and found that: "When instead of the metals, pieces of well-burned charcoal were employed, the spark was still longer, and of a vivid whiteness, an evident combustion was produced, the charcoal remained red-hot for some time after the contact, and threw off bright corruscations." Arc lighting was for long afterwards used quite widely when a vivid light was required.

AT THE ROYAL INSTITUTION

All this work brought recognition, and in 1801 Davy was invited to become Lecturer in Chemistry at the Royal Institution in London. This had recently been founded with the objectives of providing technical education for working men and of arousing an interest in science and, particularly, technology, among the leisured classes. The former objective was pursued with rather less success than the latter; and the Royal Institution became a centre of scientific research rather than a technical college. Count Rumford, the American who, after siding with the British in the War of Independence, took service under the Elector of Bavaria and rose to high office, was the leading figure in the early years of the Institution. He performed experiments with cannon-boring machinery to show that mechanical work could be transformed into heat; but in his day most scientists adhered to the caloric theory, and he was regarded as rather old-fashioned. His fame lay more in his improvements to fireplaces and stoves, and in his achievement of ending begging and unemployment in Bavaria by establishing centres where work and food were available. Rumford must have been pleased that Davy's views on heat coincided with his own; but apparently he was rather shocked on meeting Davy, who was at his appointment only twenty-two, to find him rather rustic and uncouth.

But Davy soon showed that he could take a polish, and his lectures proved an enormous success. Audiences of a thousand people flocked to hear him. The lectures make very good reading; in them, Davy went further in his speculations than in his books and published papers, and also he reported on work in progress, so the lectures have a liveliness that one might not expect of obsolete chemistry. The Professor of Chemistry was Dr. Garnett, who had come from Glasgow; but he was not as successful in London as he had been in Scotland, and also he suffered a number of personal misfortunes soon after his arrival. Davy was soon promoted in his place.

Because of Rumford's wide interests, and his especial enthusiasm for technology, Davy had to give lectures not only on chemistry but also on geology—his lectures were, he claimed, the first public ones on that subject in London—and on agriculture, dyeing, bleaching, tanning, metallurgy, and the construction of fireplaces. His agricultural lectures were published in 1813, and became a classic textbook until they were replaced in the next generation by Liebig's book. These lectures received somewhat mixed reviews, and it is not clear whether they forwarded greatly the cause of more scientific farming; but he certainly helped to arouse interest in the subject.

Davy never abandoned this interest in technology, and was prouder of his safety lamp for miners than of any of his scientific discoveries. But he always separated science and its applications, and never believed that only obviously useful lines of research should be followed. "A newly discovered country", he declared, "ought not to be neglected, though it cannot be immediately brought into cultivation, because it does not immediately produce corn, and wine, and oil." And he went on to justify disinterested scientific inquiry: "But independently of these considerations, all truths in nature, all inventions by which they can be developed, are worthy of our study for their own sake rather than with any idea of profit or interest . . . the noblest faculties are reason and the love of knowledge. . . . Man is formed for pure enjoyments; his duties are high, his destination is lofty; and he must, then, be most accused of ignorance and folly when he grovels in the dust, having wings which can carry him to the skies."

THE BAKERIAN LECTURES

In his first years at the Royal Institution, Davy found little time for continuing his electrical researches. In 1803 he was elected a Fellow of the Royal Society, then still, under the presidency of Sir Joseph Banks, made up of a majority of non-scientists. Not until Davy became President—he followed Banks who had been elected in the year Davy was born—did even the policy-making Council of the Society contain a majority of active scientists. Davy soon became one of the secretaries of the Society; and in November 1806 he was invited to deliver the Bakerian lecture to the Society. To be asked to give one of these lectures, which happen annually, is a great honour; and Davy gave five in succession between 1806 and 1810, of which three are of outstanding merit.

Davy took up electrochemistry again in 1806, and his researches with the battery formed the basis of his lecture. In 1800 he had found that electrolysis, the decomposition of a dissolved substance by electricity, would proceed quite happily even if the two metal poles through which the current entered and left the solution were in different cups. To complete the circuit the cups had to be connected, and this could be done by moistened "amianthus"—woven asbestos fibres—or even by people holding hands. Davy performed most of his experiments in 1806 with two cups, connected by amianthus bridges.

The Bakerian lecture was generally applauded; the Swedish scientist Berzelius wrote "that it must be placed among the finest memoirs with which chemical theory has been enriched", and Thomas Thomson, the leading Scottish chemist, considered it "not merely the best of all his own productions, but . . . the finest and completest specimen of inductive reasoning which appeared during the age in which he lived". Napoleon awarded Davy a medal for the discoveries announced in the lecture, and later Davy was given a special safe-conduct to go to Paris and collect the medal though Britain and France were at war.

Davy began by settling the question of what happens when an electric current is passed through water. From the first Davy seems to have been convinced that pure water would yield pure oxygen and hydrogen only; but other workers had found numerous other processes taking place. In particular, acids and alkalies seemed to be generated during electrolysis. Davy began his researches using glass apparatus—the glass usually used in chemical laboratories at this date was green bottle-glass—but he soon suspected that the glass was in some way affecting the course of the experiment. He therefore switched to vessels of agate, when the quantities of acid and alkali produced were much smaller. Whichever vessels were used, the quantities of acid and alkali were less in successive experiments; this seemed to indicate that something coming from the apparatus and not the water was responsible. The acid Davy found to be nitrous acid, and the alkali sodium carbonate. Gold vessels gave the same results as agate, so he tried redistilling his water from a silver still (the success of Davy's lectures had by now put the Royal Institution on a firm financial basis). The water indeed left a residue in the still; and the redistilled water, in agate apparatus, gave very little acid and alkali on electrolysis. On the addition of lumps of glass, more acid and alkali appeared, so Davy had established that the glass must have been dissolving to produce most of the impurities.

The alkali in the redistilled water experiment was ammonia, and Davy suspected that it and the nitrous acid might have originated in the nitrogen of the air, combining during the electrolysis with the hydrogen and the oxygen generated. So he decided to perform the experiment *in vacuo*, and on 11 November 1806 he pumped out the air from the apparatus, filled it with hydrogen again, and then evacuated it finally. No nitrogen should have remained in the apparatus after this treatment; and Davy's hypothesis that nitrogen was responsible for the acid and alkali was confirmed when, even after the current had been passing for some hours, the water remained neutral. Davy could conclude that: "It seems evident that water, chemically pure, is decomposed by electricity into gaseous matter alone, into oxygene* and hydrogene*."

This presents a textbook example of a fairly simple problem being so solved by the rigid and intelligent application of the experimental method. We find Davy doing much the same, with equal success, in his safety lamp investigation nine years later. Both investigations were carried out fast; Davy was a rapid and impulsive worker, whose laboratory tended to be disorganized. But he had the capacity for accurate and painstaking work, and for spotting possible causes of error. Later he noticed the inaccuracies that can arise from using wet apparatus, a practice usual in his day.

Not all scientific investigations can be handled in this way, though. Some problems are much more intractable, and the finding of theoretical explanations of complex phenomena is a rather different art from the solving by beautiful and crucial experiments of single problems. Davy showed himself no less capable in this

*Davy's spelling.

field. In the latter half of his lecture he turned to the theoretical problems presented by the phenomena of electrochemistry; the decomposition of insoluble substances, the transport of substances through the solution to appear only at the poles where the current enters and leaves, and the problem of why electricity breaks chemical bonds.

Davy tried to decompose insoluble substances such as calcium sulphate by making his apparatus out of them, and found that after the passage of the current sulphuric acid was indeed found in the positive cup, and calcium hydroxide in the negative one. But his attempts at quantitative analysis by this method were not very successful. More interesting were his experiments on transport. Here he tried using three vessels, and put litmus solution into all three of them. When he used calcium chloride ("muriate of lime") in the negative cup, and water in the other two, the parts of the solution round the positive and negative poles became acid and alkaline when the current was passed, but the intermediate vessel remained neutral though acid must somehow have passed through it. This was a clear experimental proof of what later was called Faraday's first law, that the action in electrolysis takes place at the poles.

Since acids could be passed through litmus in the central vessel without causing it to change colour, Davy wondered whether insoluble bodies could also be made to pass through an intermediate vessel. So he put a barium salt in the positive cup, a solution of silver sulphate in the central, and hydrochloric acid in the negative cup. But both barium sulphate and silver chloride were precipitated.

Davy's explanation of all this was somewhat tentative; a working hypothesis rather than a detailed theory. Indeed, Faraday was later able to produce no less than twelve published theories of electrolysis all claiming to be based on Davy's views, and all incompatible with one another. Davy wrote: "It is very natural to suppose, that the repellent and attractive energies are communicated from one particle to another particle of the same kind, so as to establish a conducting chain in the fluid; and that locomotion takes place in consequence. . . ." He believed that the attraction of the poles was the cause of the motion, and seems to have supposed chains of particles through the liquid. But beyond that he left the question open.

As to why electricity should decompose bodies, he had an answer. Chemical affinity and electrical energy were different manifestations of the same power. Chemical bonding was in fact electrical; so it could be broken by the application of an electrical potential to the compound. Davy's words are: "As the chemical attraction between two bodies seems to be destroyed by giving one of them an electrical state different from that which it naturally possesses, that is by bringing it into a state similar to the other, so it may be increased by exalting its natural energy. Thus whilst zinc, one of the most oxidable of the metals, is incapable of combining with oxygene when negatively electrified in the circuit, even by a feeble power; silver, one of the least oxidable, easily unites to it when positively electrified. . . . Amongst the bodies which combine chemically, all those, the electrical energies of which are well known, exhibit opposite states. . . . In the present state of our knowledge, it would be useless to attempt to speculate on the remote cause of the electrical energy or the reason why different bodies, after being brought into contact, should be found differently electrified; its relation to chemical affinity is, however, sufficiently evident. May it not be identical with it, and an essential property of matter?"

Bodies, in Davy's view, have definite electrical states; some, the metals, are positive, while others are negative. These states can be determined by touching two bodies and seeing what electrical charge they show after contact. If the weakly-positive silver is given a strong positive charge from the battery, it becomes more active chemically; and conversely, zinc, given a negative charge, becomes chemically inert. In chemical combination, positive and negative bodies combine and neutralize their charges in the process. In the hands of Berzelius this theory, which works well in inorganic chemistry but cannot satisfactorily explain the bonding between like substances characteristic of the organic branch of the subject, became the sophisticated system, "dualism", which dominated the science for a generation.

Davy had no great interest in building systems. To him, these electrical discoveries were important because a new road seemed to have been opened up leading to the analysis of substances which had hitherto resisted all attempts to break them down. Lavoisier had laid it down firmly that bodies that could not be analysed were to be treated as elements; but in fact he had not adhered rigidly to this dictum. For the alkalies, soda and potash, had not been analysed, and nor had any of the "earths", such as silica, alumina, or magnesia. Yet the analogy between the alkalies and the compound body ammonia, and between the earths and the metallic oxides, such as ferric oxide, seemed to Lavoisier to give grounds for treating these bodies as compounds and not as elements. This difficulty remained throughout the nineteenth century; many bodies were found which showed clear analogies with compound substances, and yet resisted analysis. Chemists differed over whether they ought to be regarded as elements or not; and the problem was not solved until Moseley and Bohr, in this century, were able to redefine "element" in terms of electronic structure instead of having to talk about resisting analysis.

Davy held throughout his life the view that there must be fewer genuine elements than the forty or so that were in his day known. For this reason he opposed the atomic theory put forward by his acquaintance, John Dalton; nevertheless he put Dalton up for the Royal Society, though Dalton at first refused to be nominated. Dalton supposed that the atoms of each element were different from those of all other elements, though themselves all alike. If these "atoms" were really atoms, and unsplittable, then any attempt to analyse an element would be bound to be in vain; Davy interpreted Dalton as saying this, and therefore opposed his system. In fact Dalton was not completely clear, and in some places seems to mean only that if an atom of, say, iron were split, then it would no longer be iron.

We find Davy's clearest expression of his belief in the simplicity of nature in a lecture on the chemical elements that he gave in

1809. "From the past progress of the human mind", he declared, "we have a right to reason concerning its future progress. And on this ground, a high degree of perfection may be expected in chemical philosophy. Whoever compares the complication of the systems which have been hitherto adopted, and the multitude, as it were, of insignificant elements with the usual simplicity and grandeur of nature, will surely not adopt the opinion, that the highest methods of our science are already attained; or that events so harmonious as those of the external world, should depend upon such complex and various combinations of numerous and different materials." It is ironic that this belief that the world must be made up of but few true elements should have aroused him to use the electric battery in his analyses; and that in performing these analyses he should have become one of the most prolific discoverers of new elements in all the history of chemistry.

In his second Bakerian lecture, of 1807, he announced the spectacular discovery of the elements potassium and sodium. Despite Lavoisier's doubts, most chemists seem to have regarded soda and potash as elements. In September 1807 Davy began a series of experiments designed to analyse them. He began by electrolysing solutions of potash, but obtained only oxygen and hydrogen. So he tried using solid fused potash; but this was a nonconductor. When its surface was slightly wetted, however, it did permit the current of electricity to flow, and globules of metal appeared at the negative pole, some of which burst into flames and were lost, while some remained and could be investigated. Davy danced about the room in ecstatic delight. Oxygen was given off at the other pole, so it was clear that potash had been decomposed into these globules and oxygen. In his notebook Davy wrote: "The substance is analogous to some of those imagined to exist by the alchemical visionaries."

A few days later Davy isolated sodium in the same way. The lightness of these new substances, their low melting-points—made lower because Davy's potassium was mixed with enough sodium to make it fluid at room temperature—and their extreme reactivity inclined many scientists to doubt if they were really

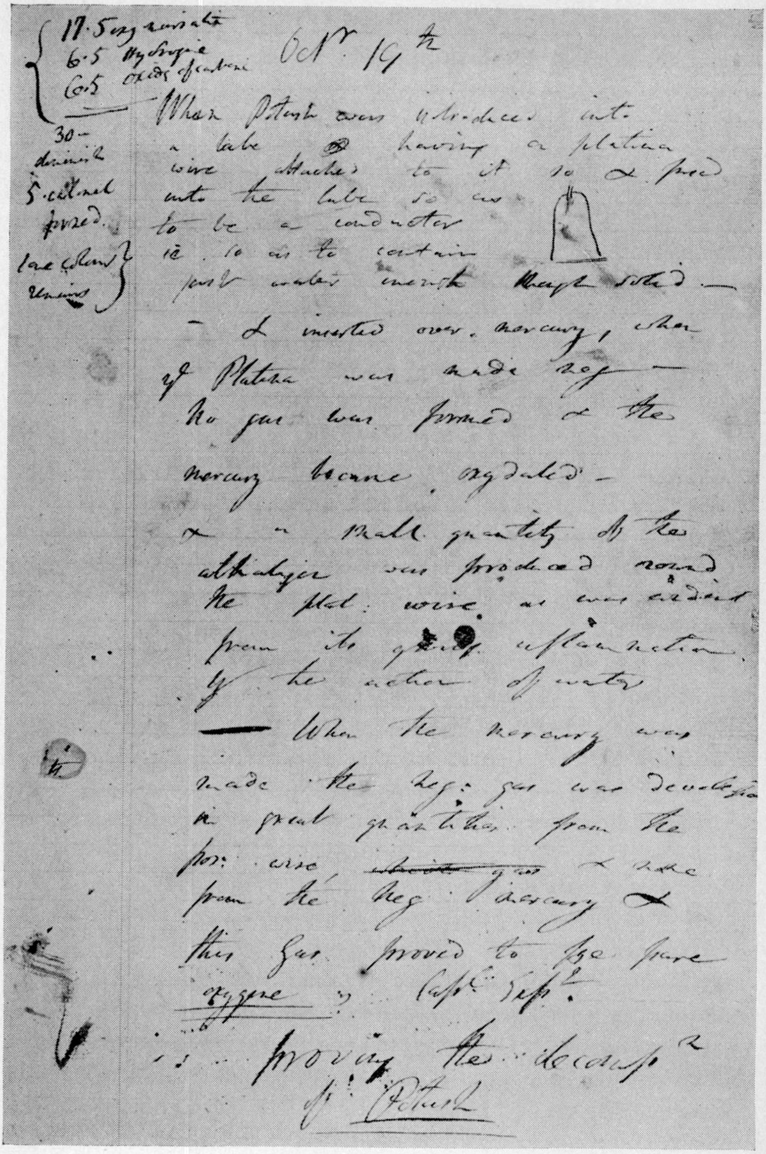

PLATE 3. Davy's notes on the electrolysis of potash.

metals, and not a few believed that they must contain hydrogen. As late as 1828 a writer declared that sodium and potassium were "little better than hypothetical assumptions", and that "nothing but the rage of the day for the invention of new metals could have prompted their insertion in the list", so different were their properties from those of ordinary metals. But Davy was firm; after toying with "sodagen" and "potagen" he came down in favour of the present names, whose ending in "um" implies metallic status. "In the philosophical division of the classes of bodies", he wrote, "the analogy between the greater number of properties must always be the foundation of arrangement."

In about two months Davy had discovered sodium and potassium, and, using the minute quantities available from his electrolytic process, had determined many of the chemical properties of these substances. The *Edinburgh Review* called the published Bakerian lecture: "the most valuable (paper) in the *Philosophical Transactions* since the time when Sir Isaac Newton inserted, in that celebrated collection, the first account of his optical discoveries." For at this time the barrier between the sciences and the humanities had not been raised to its present height; and literary reviews also commented on articles in scientific journals, and on scientific books. Perhaps because of this most scientists wrote better and for a wider public than would be the case now; or perhaps this was simply because the number of professional scientists was so few in any field. No degree courses in the sciences were available, except in medicine; and Davy was one of the very few men who made a living out of their science alone.

Davy intended to apply the battery to the earths, but he was taken ill with typhus, "gaol fever", following a visit to Newgate to suggest methods for ventilating the prison. His life was in danger, and carriages with people coming to ask after his health blocked Albemarle Street. He recovered rather slowly; and in the meantime Berzelius had succeeded in decomposing some of the alkaline earths using a negative pole of mercury which dissolved the metal as it was liberated from its oxide, as Davy had done in his isolation of potassium, when he observed oxygen coming off at the opposite pole. Berzelius also discovered something else that aroused Davy's interest: "ammonium amalgam". This can be made by electrolysing an ammonium salt using a mercury electrode, and the amalgam produced is very different from mercury and somewhat resembles sodium or potassium amalgam. About sixty years later, the American chemist Seely established that ammonium amalgam obeys Boyle's Law, which applies to gases, and that it is therefore a froth of ammonia and hydrogen in the mercury. But to Davy and his contemporaries, it appeared that the amalgam was a metallic amalgam, and that ammonium was a genuine metal like sodium and potassium. But ammonium was known to be a compound; so, by analogy, sodium, potassium, and probably most other metals too were also compounds.

Davy's Bakerian lectures of 1808 and 1809 were concerned with the applications of electricity to chemistry. He isolated and named a number of the earth metals, and also boron which he called "boracium". But during these years he was preoccupied with problems of chemical theory. The great French chemist Lavoisier, in the previous generation, had disposed of phlogiston, an entity thought to be given off when bodies burned. He established that in the process of combustion the body that was burning combined with the oxygen of the air. He also held to the caloric theory of heat; oxygen gas, according to this theory, was a compound of oxygen with caloric, caloric oxide. All gases were in fact caloric compounds; and when a body evaporated the "latent heat" that it absorbed was believed to be combining chemically with it. So combustion became a simple process: if M be the combustible body, then we have:

$$M + \text{caloric oxide} = M \text{ oxide} + \text{caloric}.$$

The caloric is simply the heat we know to be evolved in burning.

Lavoisier's synthesis contained yet another strand: his theory of acidity. He had found that many acids were produced by combustions; and he wrote: "I might multiply these experiments, and shew, by a numerous succession of facts, that all acids are formed by the combustion of certain substances. . . . In the mean time, however, the three examples already cited (carbon, sulphur and phosphorus) may suffice for giving a clear and accurate description of the manner in which acids are formed. By these it may be clearly seen, that oxygen is an element common to them all, and which constitutes or produces their acidity; and that they differ from each other, according to the several natures of the oxygenated or acidified substances. We must therefore, in every acid, distinguish between the acidifiable base, which Mr. de Morveau calls the radical, and the acidifying principle, or oxygen." The term "oxygen" indeed means generator of acids. Muriatic acid— our hydrochloric acid—had indeed caused Lavoisier a certain amount of worry. Of it he had written: "Although we have not been able, either to compose or decompose this acid of sea-salt, we cannot have the smallest doubt that it, like all other acids, is composed by the union of oxygen with an acidifiable base. We have therefore called this unknown substance the *muriatic base* or *muriatic radical*." Of chlorine, Lavoisier wrote: "In common with sulphuric acid, and several other acids, the muriatic is capable of different degrees of oxygenation, . . . an additional saturation with oxygen renders it more volatile, of a more penetrating odour, less miscible with water, and diminishes its acid properties." For Lavoisier, chlorine was oxymuriatic acid; if the acid had the formula XO, chlorine would be represented by XO_2. His equation for neutralization of a base was: acid + base = salt; ours is: acid + base = salt + water. We should call most of Lavoisier's acids "anhydrides"; sulphur trioxide, SO_3, for example, is the anhydride of sulphuric acid, H_2SO_4, and in fact it does not display acid properties if there is no water present. The modern theory of acids, that they are hydrogen compounds, originated not with Lavoisier but with Davy.

Lavoisier's view of acids was pressed with difficulties from the start, for water, a non-metallic oxide, was not an acid; to say that hydrogen was not an acidifiable base was seen to be begging the question. Hydrogen sulphide, H_2S, the well-known substance that smells of bad eggs, was an acid, and yet contained no oxygen. But chemists before Davy had no alternative suggestion to offer, in

B

place of Lavoisier's, concerning the nature of acids. Davy in 1808 toyed with the phlogiston theory again, and with the idea that all metals might contain some "principle of metallization", possibly hydrogen; this latter idea came from his experiments on the ammonium amalgam. Davy quite possibly believed these "phlogistic" notions; but his view of the role of hypotheses in chemistry was that they should not be taken too seriously, but rather used as a guide to research. At the end of one of his papers he stated that: "Hypotheses can scarcely be considered as of any value, except as leading to new experiments."

Though Davy believed that perhaps all metals might contain hydrogen, many of his experiments in 1808 were designed to establish that potassium was not a hydrogen compound. Its status, Davy succeeded in showing, was the same as that of all other metallic elements. Some new technique of analysis might— and Davy believed that it would—prove all metals to contain hydrogen, but if Lavoisier's criterion of an element was to be adhered to, then potassium was just as much an element as iron. This argument Davy then extended to chlorine. Though analogy might lead one to suspect that chlorine contained oxygen, no proof of this had been produced. Many workers had sought in vain for the basis X of muriatic acid, XO, and oxymuriatic acid, XO_2. Davy himself had tried to analyse the latter by sparking, with no result. Oxygen could only be obtained from the latter compound in the presence of water, but this was something earlier investigators had not noticed. In the absence of direct evidence that oxymuriatic acid had been decomposed, it must be regarded as an element, whose properties were similar to those of oxygen.

This step Davy took in July 1810; and he went on to make another step, this time dethroning caloric. Heat and light produced in chemical reactions, he declared, are not caloric being liberated from its combinations but represent chemical energy. He wrote: "The vivid inflammation of bodies, in oxymuriatic acid gas, at first view, appears a reason why oxygene should be admitted in it; but heat and light are merely results of the intense agency of combination". In 1810 and 1811 Davy clarified his position in a series of lectures and papers. He was severe especially to Berthollet, the French chemist who led those who continued to maintain Lavoisier's position. "The opinions of Berthollet", Davy remarked, "have been received for nearly thirty years; and no part of modern chemistry has been considered so firmly established, or so happily elucidated; but we shall see that it is entirely false—the baseless fabric of a vision. . . . Oxymuriatic acid is not an acid, any more than oxygen; but it becomes acid, like that substance, by combining with inflammable matter. . . . The confidence of the French inquirers closed for nearly a third of a century this noble path of investigation, which I am convinced will lead to many results of much more importance than those which I have endeavoured to exhibit to you. Nothing is so fatal to the progress of the human mind as to suppose that our views of science are ultimate; that there are no mysteries in nature; that our triumphs are complete, and that there are no new worlds to conquer."

At the height of the Napoleonic Wars, this polemic was popular; but when in 1813 Davy went to France to collect his medal for the first Bakerian lecture, he was well-received and most French scientists had come round to his position on chlorine. His behaviour to his hosts was not always above reproach, however. While he was in France a new substance was discovered by Courtois, which gave a violet vapour on heating. Davy investigated it, Courtois passed some to Gay-Lussac to investigate; but Davy got hold of some more, and rushed to get his conclusion, that it was an analogue of chlorine, *iodine*, published first. The discovery of this substance meant that chlorine no longer stood alone as an acidifying substance, apart from oxygen; and most chemists gave up Lavoisier's theory of acids.

One of the audience who managed to get to Davy's lectures on chlorine was a young apprentice bookbinder, Michael Faraday. He had taken an interest in science for some time, and was greatly excited by the lectures; he wrote to his friend Abbot: "I would wish you not to be surprised if the old theory of phlogiston should

be again adopted as the true one, tho' I do not think it will entirely set aside Lavoisier's, but the *Elements* (Davy's forthcoming
book) will inform you." In fact, Lavoisier's work remained the
basis of modern chemistry, though large portions of it had proved
in need of replacement or amendment. Faraday bound his notes
of the lectures, and sent them to Davy, who saw him. Faraday
declared that he wished to give up trade and follow science; Davy
told him that scientists were not as high-minded as Faraday
thought, but when this failed to deter him, Davy promised to
help. And when his laboratory assistant at the Royal Institution
was sacked for hitting an instrument-maker, he offered Faraday
the post. All Faraday's later work was done in the laboratories of
the Royal Institution, where he had served his apprenticeship
under Davy. Faraday has been called Davy's greatest discovery;
and despite some friction between them later on, when Faraday
was involved in a misunderstanding and Davy, failing to realize
that his former pupil was now an important scientist in his own
right, opposed his election to the Royal Society, Faraday always
admired Davy.

Meanwhile Davy had been knighted by the Prince Regent for
his discoveries, and had married a wealthy widow, Mrs. Apreece,
who had cut quite a figure in society. Davy's friends of Bristol days
had been alarmed lest he be corrupted by his rapid social and
scientific success; and some have seen in his marriage, after which
he did relatively little important work, evidence that he had been
so corrupted. On his marriage he resigned his post at the Royal
Institution, though he continued to lecture there, and to work in
the laboratory, in an honorary capacity. On 12 August 1812, he
wrote to his friend Clayfield: "Having given up lecturing, I shall
be able to devote my whole time to the pursuit of discovery." But
this did not happen.

In 1812 he brought out the first part of his *Elements of Chemical
Philosophy*. This part dealt mostly with his own discoveries, and
the subsequent parts, to cover the rest of the field of chemistry,
never appeared. One critic at least considered this a good thing,
for Davy would not have been able to maintain the interest and

originality of the work when he was recording other men's discoveries. Davy himself said that he could not imitate, he could only invent. Berzelius deplored the lack of a broad education in the sciences that he observed in Davy; his work, Berzelius thought, was a "brilliant fragment", and if only Davy had been made to write reviews of the whole progress of chemistry each year, as Berzelius and Thomas Thomson did, then he might have advanced the science by a century. There may be something in this; but Berzelius was quite a different kind of thinker. He was a systematizer, interested in organizing the whole field, and with rather dogmatic ideas on chemical theory. Davy was original and sparkling; he changed his theories when they did not appear to produce results; and his great discoveries came in great surges of activity, interspersed with periods of much less intensity. It is possible that a too great insistence on a firm grounding in the science might have crushed his originality.

His continental tour was marked by his experiments on iodine; he also met many foreign scientists, including Volta who had put on his best clothes to receive his distinguished guest, who arrived shabbily dressed for travelling. Davy established cordial relations with some of the French scientists, notably Ampère; but others were put off by his arrogant-seeming manner, and by the way he worked on iodine, which Gay-Lussac was known to be investigating—perhaps this was meant as a reprisal, for Gay-Lussac had entered Davy's own field by publishing research on potassium. Davy was not impressed by Napoleonic France, and on his return he wrote a memorandum to be sent to the Foreign Office advising the most rigorous policies by the occupying powers when Napoleon was overthrown. He was the only Englishman allowed to visit France, and Lady Davy's hat caused a sensation in Paris. The curious crowd that gathered was dispersed, and she was given a military escort back to her hotel. Faraday accompanied the Davys on the tour, but he was not happy; Lady Davy made him perform some of the duties of a valet, and generally treated him as a servant.

THE SAFETY LAMP

On Davy's return, he was asked by some of the coal-owners in the north-east if he could help them to solve the problem of explosions in coal-mines, which had been particularly serious in the last two or three years. There had been numerous explosions involving heavy losses of life, and a committee had been formed, of which John Buddle was the most active member. Davy visited a number of mines in August 1815, and in October a sample of "fire damp", the explosive gas, was sent to him at the Royal Institution. He found that a lamp would not cause an explosion if it were air-tight but furnished with narrow tubes to admit the air, for the cooling effect of the tubes does not permit an explosion to pass. This had been observed earlier by Tennant and Wollaston, but Davy does not seem to have known of their experiments. Fire damp, more than many other gases, requires a high temperature before its mixture with air will explode, and Davy found that metal tubes, which dissipated heat faster, were more efficient than glass for admitting air to the lamp while not allowing it to ignite the fire damp. Finally he discovered that fine metal gauze was as good as tubes and his latest lamp was encased in wire gauze. Experiments in coal-mines with the lamps established that they did not cause explosions although there was fire damp in the atmosphere. Even when the gauze was red-hot it did not ignite the gas; and moreover the character of the flame changed in the presence of fire damp, so the lamp acted as an indicator of the state of the air in the mine. Buddle took the lamp down Wall's End Colliery, and reported: "I first tried it in an explosive mixture on the surface; and then took it into a mine; . . . it is impossible for me to express my feelings at the time when I first suspended the lamp in the mine and saw it red-hot. . . . I said to those around me 'We have at last subdued this monster.' " Within a few months collieries all over the country were using the lamp, whose designs Davy published and refused to patent, though Buddle told him he might derive an income of five to ten thousand pounds from it. "More wealth", replied Davy, "would

not increase either my fame or my happiness. It might undoubtedly enable me to put four horses to my carriage; but what
would it avail me to have it said that Sir Humphry drives his
carriage and four?"

The coal-owners presented Davy with a set of gold plate, worth
£2500, in gratitude, and miners presented him with testimonials,
often signed with a mark for many of them had had no schooling.
Davy was very proud of such expressions of gratitude. Unfortunately George Stephenson, who became famous as the rail-
way engineer, had produced a safety-lamp at about the same
time. His lamp was rather like Davy's; and a committee of distinguished scientists—mostly friends of Davy's—declared it to be
an evident imitation of Davy's. It seems that Stephenson was not
fully aware of the principles behind the safety-lamp, but had
arrived at the lamp by trial and error.

The lamp was taken up abroad, and Davy received numerous
honours for the discovery. It is sad to have to record that in the
fifteen years following the invention of the lamp, colliery accidents
did not fall; indeed they showed a slight rise. The owners blamed
the colliers for being careless with the lamps, which become unsafe if battered; and the colliers blamed the owners for reopening
extremely explosive shafts now that they had the lamps. Ventila-
tion in mines also improved, and the original Davy lamp becomes unsafe in a strong draught.

Davy made another tour abroad in 1818–20, visiting mines and
attempting to unroll some papyri found at Herculaneum. In
June 1820 Sir Joseph Banks died; he had been President of the
Royal Society for 42 years. Davy, who had been made a baronet
in 1818 for his work on the lamp—a poor honour for a knight
with no children—now announced that he would be a candidate
for the presidency. Wollaston, another chemist, had been elected
acting President; but, after an interview with Davy, who had
canvassed energetically, he declared that he would not stand in
November, and at the Anniversary Meeting on St. Andrew's Day
1820, Davy was elected President of the Royal Society. After so
long a tenure of office by a distinguished and aristocratic botanist,

it is not surprising that the election of a *nouveau-riche* chemist of genius should have shaken up the Society. He wished, his brother reported, to bring the Society more into line with the institution described in Bacon's *New Atlantis*.

His tenure of office as President, however, was not wholly successful; he tried to maintain the dignity with which Banks had invested the position, but his temperament was too lively and irascible, and he quarrelled with many of his colleagues. Undoubtedly he laboured for the Society to the best of his abilities; and the hard work entailed may have contributed to the breakdown of his health. In the autumn of 1823 the mysterious disease that was to prove fatal first struck him, and after that date he was never again really well. He described his return to England after a continental tour in search of health, shortly after he had heard of his mother's death in 1824: "My health was gone, my ambition was satisfied, I was no longer excited by the idea of distinction; what I regarded most tenderly was in the grave, and, to take a metaphor, derived from the change produced by time in the grape, my cup of life was no longer sparkling, sweet, and effervescent;—it had lost its sweetness without losing its power, and it had become bitter." His ambition was not wholly satisfied, however, for in 1827 he wrote to Lady Davy: "You talk of honours; I ought to have been made a Privy Councillor and a Lord of Trade, as my predecessor was."

The despair produced by his illness was accentuated by his failure to prevent the corrosion of the copper on the bottoms of warships by attaching iron protectors to the copper sheeting. The iron, being electrically more positive than the copper, was preferentially attacked. The idea was sound; but unfortunately seaweed adhered to the protected copper, and slowed the ships up, so the experiment had to be abandoned. Cruelly witty remarks were made about this failure, which was really a sensible application of electro-chemistry that foundered on the complexity of botany.

RETIREMENT

In 1824, after attempts to cure his disease by travelling abroad had failed, he resigned the presidency of the Royal Society. In 1826 he delivered his last Bakerian lecture, which must have cost him considerable effort in his weakened condition. It adds relatively little to the electrical theories that he had advanced twenty years earlier. On the staircase at the Royal Institute there is a portrait of Davy at this period; and the contrast between this prematurely aged man and the more youthful portraits is poignant. In the spring of 1828 he again set out for the Continent; his wife remained in England. In the following March, at Rome, came a crisis; but his brother, a doctor with the forces at Malta, rushed to him, and he recovered. Lady Davy also came, from England; and in their company Davy began the journey northward. But at Geneva, on 29 May 1829, he died peacefully; he was only fifty years old.

During his retirement he wrote two works, both of which proved extremely popular. One was *Salmonia*, a work in imitation of Isaak Walton, about fly-fishing. The other was *Consolations in Travel, or the Last Days of a Philosopher*, a more serious book, unfinished at his death, composed of dialogues in which Davy left to the world his mature reflections and queries on matters of science.

This work is especially interesting for the views it contains on the nature of the chemical elements, and on atoms. In 1802, well before Dalton's atomic theory was published, Davy's syllabus of lectures to be given at the Royal Institution shows that, like most of his contemporaries, he was a corpuscularian. That is to say, he believed that bodies were made up of corpuscles, or minute particles. He wrote: "The different bodies in nature are composed of particles or minute parts, individually imperceptible to the senses. When the particles are similar, the bodies they constitute are denominated simple, and when they are different, compound. The chemical phenomena result from the different arrangement of the particles of bodies; and the powers that produce these arrangements are repulsion, or the agency of heat, and attraction." It seems odd that Davy, if he believed this, rejected the atomic theory; but most of his contemporaries did likewise.

Where Davy differed from Dalton was in refusing to believe that the chemical elements were in fact simple bodies composed of simple particles. Potassium closely resembles ammonium, known to be a compound; and chlorine has properties very like those of cyanogen, composed of carbon and nitrogen. Davy had established that these elements had as good a right to be on the list as any, and the chemical world agreed with him. Arguments from their analogy with compounds could therefore be extended to cover all the elements. And if it were argued that the properties of the elements were so different as to make it unlikely that they were all composed of some few real elements, Davy could point to the difference between air, laughing gas, and the poisonous, acidic nitric oxide, which all consist of oxygen and nitrogen in different proportions.

But this was not Davy's only reason for disagreeing with Dalton. Like many of his contemporaries, he felt—and with some justice— that Dalton had gone too far beyond the facts in his little diagrams of atoms. It was one thing to use atoms as Newton had done to explain expansion and contraction by heat, and other phenomena of physics, and quite another to seek to explain the combination of substances in definite proportions by what a later critic called "scribbled pictures". Davy, as President of the Royal Society, made the speech when Dalton was awarded a royal medal for his researches. The medal, said Davy, was awarded to Dalton "for the development of the chemical theory of definite proportions, usually called the Atomic Theory, and for his various other labours and discoveries in physical and chemical science. . . . He first laid down, clearly and numerically, the doctrine of multiples; and endeavoured to express, by simple numbers, the weights of the bodies believed elementary. His first views from their boldness and peculiarity, met with but little attention; but they were discussed and supported by Drs. Thomson and Wollaston; and the table of chemical equivalents of this last gentleman, separates the practical part of the doctrine from the hypothetical part, and is worthy of the profound views and philosophical acumen and accuracy of the celebrated author. . . . With respect to the weight or quantity in which the different elementary substances entered into union to form compounds, there were scarcely any distinct or accurate data. Persons whose names had high authority, differed considerably in their statements of results; and statical chemistry, as it was taught in 1799, was obscure, vague and indefinite, not meriting the name of a science. To Mr. Dalton belongs the distinction of first unequivocally calling the attention of philosophers to this important subject . . . thus making the statics of chemistry depend upon simple questions, in subtraction or multiplication, and enabling the student to deduce an immense number of facts from a few well-authenticated, accurate, experimental results."

Wollaston, whose researches on the proportions in which bodies combine had confirmed that they do so in definite and multiple proportions, had decided that the supposition of atoms was no help in explaining this. Such atoms were purely theoretical entities, and it was better not to introduce them and instead simply to accept that bodies combine in fixed proportions by weight, which Wollaston called "equivalents". This problem still causes some confusion in fourth-form chemistry; and until the rise of structural organic chemistry, from about 1870, many chemists followed Wollaston and rejected atomic explanations.

Later in life Davy did not wholly reject atoms, but his atoms were rather different from Dalton's little spheres. Davy, followed in this by Faraday, took up the Boscovich atom, named after its proposer, an eighteenth-century Yugoslavian Jesuit. This atom was simply a mathematical point from which spheres of attractive and repulsive forces emanated. While a billiard-ball atom has a definite outside, Boscovich atoms extend their forces, getting weaker and weaker, throughout space. Also, Boscovich thought that he could build the whole world from one kind of atom. Nature is a library; different bodies are different books; chemical analysis reveals the words, and then the elements, or letters of the alphabet; but these letters are composed of identical little black points, the atoms.

Davy wrote of the "sublime chemical speculation, sanctioned by the authority of Hooke, Newton, and Boscovich, (which) must not be confused with the ideas advanced by the alchemists." In his terms, this speculation was: "There is no impossibility in the supposition that the same ponderable matter in different electrical states, or in different arrangements, may constitute substances chemically different." Davy explored these ideas in a dialogue which was unfinished at his death, and therefore was not published in the *Consolations*. So his latest ideas on the simplicity, economy, and uniformity of nature were not available as he had intended, and some later chemists failed to understand his views on the chemical elements.

We have now followed Davy in his rise from humble beginnings to a position of great importance and great fame. The belief that unified his scientific work seems to have been that the world was simple and hence composed of few elements; possibly only one kind. He deserves to be mentioned in connection with Prout's hypothesis, that all matter is made up of hydrogen. Prout based this hypothesis on Davy's ideas, and on some of Davy's experiments too; but Prout made the hypothesis more down-to-earth and testable than Davy ever did.

Before leaving Davy, let us finally note his views on the education proper for a scientist. "As the most active agents", he wrote in the *Consolations*, "are fluids, elastic fluids, heat, light, and electricity, he ought to have a general knowledge of mechanics, hydronamics, pneumatics, optics and electricity. Latin and Greek among the dead languages, and French among the modern languages are necessary; and as the most important after French, German and Italian. In natural history and in literature, what belongs to a liberal education such as that of our Universities, is all that is required. . . ." It is odd to remember that Dalton, Faraday and Davy himself, all lacked this kind of education! Certain "intellectual qualities" also were required: "Amongst them patience, industry, and neatness in manipulation, and

accuracy and minuteness in observing and registering the phenomena which occur are essential. A steady hand and a quick eye
are useful auxiliaries; but there have been few great chemists who
have preserved these advantages through life, for the business of
the laboratory is often a service of danger. . . . Both the hands and
eyes of others however may sometimes advantageously be made
use of. By often repeating a process or an observation, the errors
connected with hasty operations or imperfect views are annihi-
lated; and provided the assistant has no preconceived ideas of his
own, and is ignorant of the object of his employer in making the
experiment, his simple and bare detail of facts will often be the
best foundation for an opinion."

The plates are reproduced by kind permission of the Royal
Institution.

FURTHER READING

Davy's Bakerian lectures on the alkali metals and on chlorine are reprinted in
part in Alembic Club reprints, numbers VI and IX. Most of his papers are in
Nicholson's Journal and in the *Philosophical Transactions of the Royal Society*. They
were reprinted in his *Collected Works*, edited by his brother, 9 vols., 1839–40.
There are many biographies; the most recent are A. TRENEER, *The Mercurial
Chemist*, London, 1963, and Sir H. HARTLEY, F.R.S., *Sir Humphry Davy*, London,
in press.

CHAPTER 2

JONS JACOB BERZELIUS, 1779–1848

"WHEN a man who is endowed with exceptional talents as an investigator enriches every branch of his science with the most pregnant facts, distinguishes himself equally in empirical and speculative research, and grasps the whole subject in a philosophic spirit; when he arranges each detail systematically and clearly, and gives to the whole world a doctrinal system, critically sifted and put in as perfect a form as possible; lastly, when he proves himself a noble example of a practical and theoretical teacher to a circle of pupils eager for knowledge—that man so fulfils the highest demands of his science, that he will continue to shine forth as a brilliant model for ages to come."

This appreciation, part of the "Memorial Speech to Berzelius" delivered to the Berlin Academy in 1851 by Heinrich Rose, himself a famous chemist, and a pupil of Berzelius, testifies to the respect which the Swedish chemist inspired amongst scientists. For almost forty years he was the most distinguished chemist in the world. His *Textbook of Chemistry* was recognized as being definitive and came out in five separate editions. His pre-eminence was so assured that for the last twenty years of his life he himself wrote an annual report on the progress of physics and chemistry, in which he surveyed the whole field of science and majestically declared what he thought was important and worthwhile among all the discoveries in the world. He lived in an age when it was possible to keep in touch with developments in a wide range of subjects, and his own researches led him into physics, medicine, botany, and minerology, as well as chemistry.

In many ways to follow the work of Berzelius is to follow the progress of chemistry at the beginning of the nineteenth century, for not only did Berzelius himself make important contributions to almost every field of research, but he was also constantly engaged in argument and discussion with the other great chemists on the most interesting topics of that time. Chemistry a hundred and fifty years ago bore little resemblance to the subject as we know it today. When Berzelius started his researches there were no laboratories in Europe where one could learn practical techniques. Many universities held science lectures, but most of the work was done by private individuals, working alone. There were no international conventions where scientists might meet to discuss their work. The only means of keeping abreast of work in progress was by correspondence or personal visits, both of which proved hazardous, lengthy and expensive.

In this environment it was generally only the well-to-do who could afford the time and energy to study chemistry. Yet in spite of all these difficulties, the first twenty-five years of the nineteenth century were among the most exciting that chemistry has ever seen. During this time chemistry was at last made quantitative, rather than qualitative. Scientists measured and weighed, rather than looked and conjectured. This change of attitude led to tremendous progress in inorganic and electrochemistry, and laid the foundations of organic chemistry. Progress was so rapid that in his own lifetime Berzelius himself built up, from nothing, an almost monolithic theory of chemical reactivity, and, in his later years, he saw much of his work questioned, and later disregarded. New ideas were springing up so fast that it was impossible for him to keep in the vanguard all his life, and as he grew older he became more conservative, and clung to opinions which were by then outdated.

To discuss his entire life would be beyond the scope of this chapter. We must confine ourselves to an examination of the work of Berzelius with respect to the atomic theory, electrochemistry, and his reform of nomenclature.

HIS EARLY LIFE

Jöns Jakob Berzelius was born in Väfversunda (East Gotland) in 1779. His father was a schoolteacher, but he died four years after his son's birth, and the mother a few years later. So the young orphan went to work on his stepfather's farm. The family were very poor, and for many years the boy lived in a potato shed adjoining the farm. Little is known of his childhood, but at school he seems to have developed a love of nature study, and also of shooting.

In 1798 he went to the University of Uppsala to study medicine. While he was there his enthusiasm seems to have been more obvious than his brilliance. He even worked secretly at night in the professor's laboratory, until he was caught. After this he had to work in his lodgings.

He was eager to try out new ideas and techniques. In 1800 Volta had invented the pile, which gave a continuous current of electricity, and news of this spread quickly. In the summer of 1801, in order to pay for his university fees, Berzelius took up a temporary post as doctor to the poor at a Swedish health resort. While he was there he analysed the waters of the spa, and constructed a voltaic pile from sixty zinc plates and sixty copper coins. This work became the thesis for his doctor's degree, and, consciously or not, it set a pattern for almost all his future investigations. Throughout the rest of his life, Berzelius was mainly concerned with the analysis of compounds, and the relations between electricity and chemistry.

After he had become a doctor, Berzelius settled down in Stockholm, as a badly paid physician. There he came into contact with Hisinger, a wealthy mine owner, who gave him several rooms for research. The two men began the task of "Finding the laws according to which chemical reactions take place in the voltaic pile". They published their researches in 1803, but these did not become widely known until sixteen years later. Had the work been recognized earlier, Berzelius and Hisinger would have shared the prize awarded to Davy by the French Academy.

Berzelius was still very poor, and in order to get some money he went into business as an industrial chemist. His ventures included the manufacture of sulphuric acid, mineral water, and finally vinegar, but they all ended disastrously. In fact it took Berzelius ten years to pay back all his debts, and at one time he had to work as a labourer to earn money.

However, in 1806 he was appointed lecturer in chemistry at Karlsberg University, and in the following year he became professor at the Chirurgical School in Riddarholm. He was then reasonably well paid, and he implemented his income further by writing first a textbook on physiological chemistry, and then the first edition of his famous *Textbook of Chemistry* in 1808. Henceforward he began to devote himself to the enormous task of finding experimental evidence for the atomic theory.

THE ATOMIC THEORY

The atomic theory, in which matter is regarded as made up of discrete particles called atoms, is so fundamental to our present scientific thinking that it requires some imagination to realize that it has not always been obvious. However, we are not concerned here with the long and interesting struggle between the atomists and those who believed that matter is continuous. We are concerned with how the atomic theory was put forward, and the evidence which led people to accept it.

The atomic theory is usually linked with the name of John Dalton. This Quaker, living in Manchester, was the first to postulate that there were atoms, and then to follow this up with cogent reasons for his postulate. It is probable that Dalton was originally led to think about atoms through his work on gases, especially on partial pressures. The first account of the atomic theory appeared in print in 1807, and it postulated that:

1. Chemical elements are composed of atoms. These are minute, indivisible particles, which are not changed by chemical reactions.

2. The atoms of any one element are identical in every respect, especially weight. The weight of the atom is characteristic of the element.

3. Chemical combinations occur by the union of the atoms, in simple numerical relations, e.g. 1 atom of A + 1 atom of B; 1 atom of A + 2 atoms of B.

Dalton supported these propositions by quoting the laws of constant, multiple, and equivalent proportions.

The law of constant proportions states that the proportion by weight of elements in any compound is always the same, no matter how it is prepared. This is because it is always composed of the same number of atoms.

The law of multiple proportions states that when two elements combine to form more than one compound, the weights of one element which unite with identical weights of the other are in simple multiple proportions. This is because an atom of one element can only combine with a small whole number of atoms of another element, i.e. AB or AB_2 or AB_3.

The law of equivalent (or reciprocal) proportions states that if two elements A and B separately combine with a third C, then for a given weight of C in each, the ratio of the weights A and B will be the same as in the compound of A and B. This again is because the atoms of each element can only combine with a fixed, small number of atoms from another element.

The atomic theory was first put forward in Thomson's *System of Chemistry*, and a year later Dalton himself published it in his *New System of Chemical Philosophy*. He established the law of multiple proportions by experiments on nitrogen oxides and marsh gas.

Berzelius began to do an exhaustive analysis of many compounds before he heard of Dalton's theory. When he did hear of it he was very sceptical at first, but he realized that if it was true it was of the greatest importance. He decided that "the confirmation of Dalton's hypothesis seemed to be the greatest step that chemistry, as a science, would have made during the whole time of its existence". In thinking this he was remarkably accurate.

There were two main difficulties which prevented the ready acceptance of Dalton's theory. One was the poor quality of Dalton's own experimental work. The other difficulty was more fundamental. Although atoms combine in small whole numbers, Dalton had no way of finding out what the whole numbers were, i.e. whether a compound was AB or AB_2 or AB_3. Thus there was no way of finding out the relative weights of the atoms, e.g. in water the ratio by weight of oxygen to hydrogen is 8:1, if water is HO and the atomic weight of hydrogen is 1, then the atomic weight of oxygen is 8; but if water is H_2O and the atomic weight of hydrogen is 1 then the atomic weight of oxygen is 16.

Dalton himself tried to circumvent this difficulty by postulating a rule of simplicity, by which if only one compound were known between elements A and B then the compound would be AB. If two compounds existed then one would be AB and the other A_2B or AB_2. But this was not a scientific argument; it was a convenience designed to get Dalton out of a difficult position, because the atomic theory, no matter how elegant, was not much use to chemists until the relative weights of all the atoms could be ascertained. Only by the *measurement* of the weight could useful results be drawn up. Dalton tried to compile a list of atomic weights using hydrogen as the base, but it collapsed straight away, as he had to assume that water had a constitution HO, and this, as we have seen, led to a wrong value for the atomic weight of oxygen. This was most unfortunate as it is through oxygen that the atomic weights of most of the other elements are found, and so Dalton's table was useless.

Berzelius saw these problems, and set out to put the atomic theory on a sound, scientific footing, and also to solve the problem of how to find atomic weights.

ATOMIC WEIGHTS

First of all Berzelius established some more facts which pointed to the likely truth of the atomic theory; the proportion of sulphur to metal in metallic sulphides was the same as that in the corresponding sulphates; the amounts of oxygen in the equivalents of bases were likewise the same; and in salts of every kind the ratios between the quantities of base, acid and water were simple ones—and so on. In the years between 1812 and 1816 he investigated the oxidation of most metals and metalloids then known, and confirmed the law of multiple proportions.

Another corroboration of the atomic theory was the law of volumes enunciated by Gay-Lussac in 1808. This states that in reactions between gases the volume ratios of the reactants and products are always simple whole numbers. The classic example of this is in the formation of water:

2 volumes of hydrogen + 1 volume of oxygen = 2 volumes of water.

Strangely enough Dalton dismissed this evidence on the grounds that the results were not really accurate, but Berzelius saw that it was the first step to the table of atomic weights. He assumed that one volume of any gas contained the same number of atoms or molecules. This was enunciated by Avagadro in Italy in 1811, but was generally ignored until almost 1860. There is no evidence that Berzelius had read about Avagadro, and we must assume that he thought of this independently. Thus in the equation above, if we divide by the number of atoms or molecules in a volume we get the equation:

2 atoms of hydrogen + 1 atom of oxygen = 2 molecules of water.

But this means that 1 atom of oxygen is split into two, to get 2 molecules of water, and in Dalton's famous phrase, "Thou canst not cut an atom." So there must be at least two atoms of oxygen, making a molecule, and similarly for hydrogen. In this case the equation becomes:

2 molecules of hydrogen + 1 molecule of oxygen = 2 molecules of water.

Then, if there are the same number of atoms in a molecule of oxygen as of hydrogen, the molecule of water must have two atoms of hydrogen to every one of oxygen. The formula is H_2O. Since the ratio of oxygen to hydrogen is 8:1, the ratio for the weights of the atoms is 16:1.

It is important to realize here that all Berzelius was trying to do was to find out the weight of the atoms relative to hydrogen. He was not trying to find out the absolute weight of an individual atom. This was something which only came much later.

The method of finding the relative atomic weights from the volumes in gaseous reactions is applicable to all the elements which form gaseous compounds. Thus Berzelius was able to produce, in 1818, a table of atomic weights, which was remarkably accurate for those elements which could be vaporized, and the results are close to present-day estimates. But for other elements, and especially the metals, which do not form many gaseous compounds, many of the results were largely guesswork. Berzelius also refused to allow the combinations of 2:3, 2:5, and 3:4, which meant that he had the wrong values for all the trivalent, and many of the multivalent metals, like iron, chromium, tin, and lead.

However, in the following year, 1819, two important discoveries in physical chemistry helped to clear up these uncertainties. The first of these was Dulong and Petit's Law, which stated that for most solid elements, especially the metals, the product of the atomic weight and the specific heat is a constant, around $6 \cdot 3$. This was an empirical law, i.e. one for which there was no theoretical explanation. Dulong and Petit discovered it using fairly unreliable methods on substances of doubtful purity, but the law has stood up to later, more accurate work, and it was very useful as a generalization.

We may well ask how Dulong and Petit could be so certain of their result, since the atomic weight of most elements was in dispute. The answer is that the law was by no means certain, and was not even universally applicable, but the atomic weights of many of the more common metals was agreed on. Berzelius studied the oxides of the metals, since he knew the atomic weight of oxygen. From analysis he found the weight of the metal which combined with the atomic weight of oxygen, and he assumed that only one atom of the metal was present in the oxide. This is the reason, as we noticed, why he was wrong about the atomic weights of the trivalent metals like iron and chromium. So Dulong and Petit's law was not a certainty, which Berzelius could use with impunity. At best it was a rough guide, useful for cross checking his results, and getting values for metals where analysis was difficult. It is worth stressing that Berzelius was feeling his way in the dark, and that he had only his own judgement to tell him what information was useful to him, and how far he could rely on Gay-Lussac's Law and the work of Dulong and Petit.

In 1819 Berzelius visited France, Switzerland, and Germany, and it was on this trip that he learned of the second discovery which was to help him in his table of atomic weights. In Germany he met a young chemist called Eilhard Mitserlich, whose paper on the chrystallography of arsenates and phosphates, which later led to the law of isomorphism, impressed Berzelius greatly. Isomorphism is the term used when the crystals of two compounds are so alike that when a crystal of one is placed in a supersaturated solution of the other, the second compound grows onto the first crystal. This produces a final crystal whose centre consists of one compound and outside of another. Only crystals which are very similar will do this, among them arsenates, and phosphates with the same number of molecules of water of crystallization.

Thus Mitserlich had discovered a relation between chemical composition and crystal structure. Other examples of isomorphism were soon found, including sulphates and selenates, and iron, chromium and aluminium salts. The way in which this helped Berzelius is as follows. Suppose we want to know the atomic weight of arsenic. We already know the atomic weight of phosphorus, as it has many compounds which are gaseous, and can be analysed by Gay-Lussac's Law. We also know that phosphates are isomorphous with arsenates. First we analyse the phosphate, and find out how many grams of the other elements combine with the atomic weight of phosphorus in grams. Let us say that this is y grams. Then we take an isomorphous arsenate. We find out, by analysis, how many grams of arsenic combine with y grams of the rest of the crystal. Since we know the composition of the rest of the crystal is identical in each case, then the weight of arsenic must be its atomic weight in grams.

Using the results obtained by these two further laws Berzelius published a revised table of atomic weights in 1826. The values which he obtained are remarkably close to those in use today, the only major difference being in the alkali metals, which cannot be approached by any of the methods we have outlined. Berzelius' accuracy is due firstly to his painstaking and thorough work. In all Berzelius analysed over two thousand compounds. In order to analyse them he had to prepare them, and also to purify them. In many cases he had to work out both a method of preparation and a method of analysis, and in some cases he had to repeat analyses twenty or thirty times before he was satisfied with the result. All this he did in his inadequate laboratory, with the minimum of equipment.

In those years of routine analysis he worked out laboratory techniques which were to become standard in future years. Among the apparatus which he pioneered at this time were rubber tubing, water baths, gravimetric filter papers, the blow-pipe, and its associated reagents. Berzelius was the first person to divide the elements into groups for chemical analysis. In organic chemistry, too, he made many improvements. He evolved a standard method for the analysis of organic compounds, the results of which showed that the atomic theory was applicable to them, and this paved the way for a study of organic chemistry.

In addition to his thoroughness the accuracy of his results depended on his own good judgement. All the facts known to Berzelius were available to other chemists, but only he produced such a consistent and accurate table of atomic weights. As Lothar Meyer said, "In choosing stoichiometrical quantities to be set up as atomic weights he used all the auxiliary means at his disposal, such as analogy in chemical behaviour, density in the gaseous state, isomorphism, and specific heat, to be sure, none of these with absolute consistency, but with such delicacy of perception that with some few exceptions our currently accepted atomic weights are essentially still those of Berzelius."

Berzelius chose oxygen as his standard, partly because he believed that it was especially significant, and partly because hydrogen combines with so few elements. Through his enormous labours, Berzelius undoubtedly set the atomic theory on its feet, and made it almost universally acceptable. Whereas Dalton was perhaps one of the last of a breed of chemists who could afford to be poor at experimental work, Berzelius rightly saw that if the atomic theory was to be of any use it would have to be established by proofs from experiment, and by measurement.

It is a sad postscript to this work that, within a few years, his table of atomic weights was largely discredited. This was due to the work of Dumas, who used a vapour-density method to obtain the atomic weights of elements like iodine and sulphur. He obtained values which differed from those of Berzelius, as these substances dissociate on heating. Because of the different results, different values for the atomic weights could be used, and these proliferated throughout Europe. Confusion over atomic weights continued until 1858, when, at a conference in Karlsruhe, the Italian chemist Cannizzaro popularized the hypothesis of Avagadro, that gaseous elements were in the form of diatomic molecules. This meant that once again Gay-Lussac's Law could be used as a reliable guide to atomicity.

Meanwhile Berzelius had not forgotten his interest in electricity, and its relation to chemistry.

DUALISM

Around the beginning of the nineteenth century there was widespread interest among chemists as to the relation between electricity and chemical combination. Some spectacular results had been achieved using the voltaic pile, notably the determination of the constitution of water by electrolysis, and the isolation of the alkali metals. As we have seen, Berzelius and Hisinger investigated the action of electricity on a number of solutions, and published their work in 1803. They noted that salts decomposed by an electric current into acids and bases; that the metals go to the negative pole, and oxygen and the acids go to the positive pole; and that the extent of decomposition depends on the amount of electricity which has passed. However, in this last observation they did not properly distinguish between the E.M.F. and the current. The paper shows that Berzelius had made at least as much progress as Davy at this time, but his work was largely ignored, and he did not receive the credit for it until much later.

Both Davy and Berzelius realized that there was a very close connection between chemical combinations and electrical affinity, and they both suggested explanations. Davy's theory is rather obscure, but he believed that electricity is produced when different compounds come into contact and he suggested that chemical affinity and electrical energy are identical properties of matter (see pp. 15–16). But where Davy was cautious Berzelius was bold. To Berzelius all chemical changes were electrical changes, and with characteristic thoroughness he expanded this theme into a theory which embraced all chemical change. This was the theory of Dualism.

The outlines of this theory were first published in 1811, but the theory was not developed and fully explained until later, in *The Theory of Chemical Proportions*. In it he says, "Experience shows that heat is disengaged in every chemical combination when carried out in circumstances favourable to its perception and that by the saturation of powerful affinities the temperature often rises to the point of incandescence, whilst the satisfaction of the feeblest affinities is capable only of raising the temperature through a few degrees". Another way to obtain heat is by an electric spark or current and so "the question arises whether the union of opposite electricities is not the cause of ignition in chemical combinations as well as in the electric discharge". His conclusion is that, "In the present state of our knowledge the most probable explanation for combustion and of the ignition resulting from it is that in every chemical combination there is a neutralisation of opposite electricities."

So chemical combination is caused by the neutralization of opposite charges. The atoms of the elements are themselves electric, and electricity is a fundamental property of matter. The atoms contain both positive and negative electricity, and so they are polarized. But they do not contain equal amounts of each charge, so that they are either all positively polarized or negatively polarized. It is easy to find out what charge is on the atoms. In electrolysis if they go to the negative electrode (metals) then they are positively charged. If they go to the positive electrode (non-metals) then they have an excess of negative electricity.

Chemical combination is the attraction of the dissimilar poles of the atoms, resulting in a partial neutralization of their charge. But since the elements all carry different charges there is rarely an exact neutralization. Some residual charge is left on the compound and this may unite with another compound of opposite charge, although this second combination will be less strong.

Electrolysis is the reverse of combination. Electricity is fed into the compounds, loosening their bonds. The free elements are then liberated, and move towards the oppositely charged pole. When they arrive there they are either released or they react with the electrode or with water.

It is also possible to draw up a table, showing which elements have the largest positive charge, and which the greatest negative charge. If an element with a positive charge is compounded with one with a negative charge, and the final compound still has a positive excess charge, then the first element is higher up in the table than the second, i.e. it is more electropositive. In order to draw up the table Berzelius had to use a standard, and in order to correlate all the other elements his standard had to be either the most electropositive or the most electronegative element, by which all the others would be judged. Berzelius chose oxygen, and claimed that it was the most electronegative element. All other elements were electropositive to it, and so were above it in the table. The relative positions of the other elements were determined by compounds of the elements with oxygen. Elements which formed strong acids with oxygen were very electropositive, as they not only neutralized the negative charge but they imparted a strong residual positive charge of their own to the oxide. After this came the weaker acids, then the amphoteric oxides, then the weak bases, and so on. The final table was like this:

O, S, N, F, Cl, Br, I, Se, P, As, Cr, Mo, W, B, C, Sb, Te, Ta, Ti, Si, H, Au, Os, Ir, Pt, Rh, Pd, Hg, Ag, Cu, U, Bi, Sn, Pb, Cd, Co, Ni, Fe, Zn, Mn, Ce, Th, Zr, Al, Y, Be, Mg, Ca, Sr, Ba, Na, K.

All the elements before hydrogen are electronegative, and all coming after it are electropositive. This order is very similar to the one we use today for electrode potential, or, rather more doubtfully, for electronegativity, except that F is before O and Cl before N. In Berzelius' own words, "By arranging the atoms in the order of their electrical affinites one forms an electrochemical system which, in my opinion, is more suitable than any other arrangement to give an idea of chemistry." But he was clever enough not to suggest that this was the order of affinity of all the elements, which chemists had been searching for in their affinity tables. The affinity of the elements for oxygen varies with the temperature, e.g.

at low temperatures $2K + CO = K_2O + C$
at high temperatures $K_2O + C = CO + 2K$

Thus every body consist of two parts, which are electrically different. Without such a difference a chemical compound could not be formed, and the constitution of the substance was known when its positive and negative constituents were known. This is the doctrine of Dualism. The elements which combine with oxygen form the positive constituents, and oxygen itself is the negative one. It is easiest to see how this system worked by the following scheme, in which each downward arrow represents a reaction. The electrical polarities are given above each element.

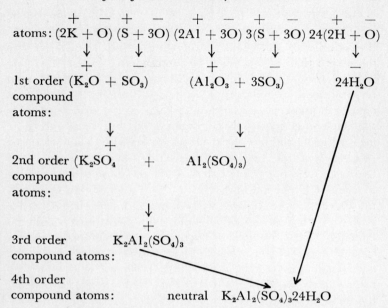

The residual charge on each of the compound atoms gets less and less going down the page, as the charges are more nearly neutralized.

In the theory of Dualism Berzelius had rationalized all the scattered facts of reaction mechanisms and brought them into one coherent system. In order to find why a compound had reacted, or to predict if it would react it was only necessary to sort out the positive and negative components. He not only did this, but in the electrochemical series he compared the charges on the elements, and gave a scale of reactivity. For twenty years this was unquestioned in Europe as a satisfactory explanation for all reaction. It is important to note the central point that the atomic theory plays here. Dualism would have been unthinkable without atoms. Indeed the very point of the theory *is* that electricity is a property of matter and is always present. This directly contradicted Davy's theory that electricity was only produced when compounds came in contact.

Gradually however facts came to light which could not be explained easily on the theory of Dualism. Once again it was through the work of Dumas, although this time his evidence was more sure than it was when he attacked the system of atomic weights. Dumas found, in organic chemistry, that chlorine could be substituted for hydrogen in acetic acid without any significant change in properties. According to Dualism it was inconceivable that such an electronegative element as chlorine could substitute for hydrogen without there being a significant change in the properties of the resulting compound, because chlorine and hydrogen were oppositely polarized, or they would not combine to form HCl. The new discovery was such a serious contradiction that Berzelius corresponded with Dumas in an effort to refute his evidence. This correspondence did not reflect much credit on Berzelius, and it resulted in Dualism being abandoned both in organic and inorganic chemistry. In inorganic chemistry it did not explain why certain acids, like hydrochloric acid, which do not contain oxygen were stronger than acids containing oxygen, the most electronegative element. Nor did it explain why molecules like N_2 or O_2 could be formed, a proposition necessary for Avagadro's hypothesis.

Thus in his old age, Berzelius saw his two most important pieces of work, the table of atomic weights, and Dualism, fall into disrepute. It is undoubtedly true that to abandon these was to hinder the progress of chemistry; the atomic weights were largely accurate, and the dualistic system has reappeared in modern theories of inorganic chemistry. That this part of his work came to be disregarded must be attributed to the dogmatic attitude adopted by Berzelius, especially the important position which he gave to oxygen in Dualism, but together they are certainly two of the most impressive contributions to chemistry up to that time.

In developing the atomic theory, and arranging a consistent table of atomic weights, Berzelius made the theory quantitative and thereby more effective. The arrangement of elements by their atomic weights prepared the ground for the classification of the elements, and later to the Periodic Table. However, it did more than this. An objection to the atomic theory had always been that there was no explanation for the elements, and that there was no limit to their number. Once Berzelius had proved that the elements did differ in weight, and once he had found out how they differed, then one reason for the existence of elements was that the weight of the atoms was different. Although this was not an explanation of why there were atoms, it was a reasonable explanation of the existence of elements, once atoms were assumed.

In Dualism Berzelius had done even more. To find out why some things react to form compounds and others do not is one of the obvious, basic questions of chemistry. Previous explanations had not been scientific; they had assumed that the atoms had human characteristics and could "love" each other, or were attracted; or that there was a mysterious force called "affinity" which bound the two elements or compounds together. Berzelius' explanation was neither of these. His views were suggested by experiment, and they could be tested against future reactions. For most of inorganic chemistry they were perfectly adequate, but in organic chemistry they did not apply, and so were eventually replaced by other explanations. This does not mean that Berzelius' explanation was necessarily correct in inorganic chemistry, but with all the facts at his disposal at that time, it was the most comprehensive explanation of a large number of apparently isolated phenomena, and that is one of the main criteria for a successful theory. After Berzelius, chemists could no longer return to speak of compounds or atoms as though they were human, and "loved" each other. Future explanation had to fit the facts, and also predict other reactions which would occur.

It is undoubtedly true that after the fall of Dualism there was widespread scepticism among many chemists. Dualism was so impressive a structure that many people, including Berzelius, thought that it could never be replaced. The facts of the newly investigated organic chemistry, which led to the downfall of Dualism, did not seem to fit into any easy pattern of thought. There was nothing so ambitious and so comprehensive to replace it. For many years after this chemists thought that all theoretical ideas were useless, and were not truly scientific. They thought that the task of the scientist was to uncover the facts, and that the facts would speak for themselves. Scepticism spread even to the atomic theory, which was not universally accepted until after 1870.

The ideas of Berzelius seem to have been disregarded as much by historical accident as by scientific reasoning. The main reason was the growth, and teething troubles of organic chemistry. The one piece of work which was not disregarded was the electro-chemical series, an important classification of the elements by their electrochemical properties.

NOMENCLATURE

The history of chemical nomenclature is intimately connected with the progress of chemistry. In most cases to apply a name to something is not just a convenient way of talking about it. Naming embraces how you think of the object, and how you classify it. This is nowhere more obvious than in chemistry.

In early chemistry, as today, when a new substance was isolated it had to be given a name. Today we have an internationally recognized way of naming new compounds, so that any chemist in the world will recognize it. Until the end of the eighteenth century this was not the case. Anyone who discovered a new compound could give it any name he chose. Clearly this practice led to considerable confusion, and there were frequently two or three names for the same compound. Nevertheless, naming was not entirely haphazard. There were certain rules which most people unconsciously obeyed, and one of these was to name the new compound by describing one of its most obvious physical characteristics.

Colour was the most obvious of these, and the etymologies of haematite (blood-like substance), orpiment (gold pigment), and verdigris (green of Greece), all relate to their colour. Colour also distinguished metals, as in plumbum candidum (white lead, i.e. tin) and plumbum nigrum (black lead, i.e. lead). Another physical property commonly used was based on consistency, or crystalline form, for instance milk of lime, and butter of antimony. Another of these was flowers of phosphorus, and perhaps the most important was spiritus for oil, as in spiritus vitrioli, and spiritus sulphuris. Taste and smell were used less frequently, one example being sugar of lead.

Apart from physical properties, there were other ways of naming substances which were more accidental, or more obscure. All the planets were associated with the earliest metals known, although at different times metals were associated with different planets. A substance might be named after the person who discovered it, a practice which was not always discouraged by the discoverer himself. Examples are Glauber's salt, and powder of Algaroth. Place names were also associated with compounds, but one of the most popular terminologies was based on the (supposed) medicinal property of the substance. Finally names might be derived from the method of preparation of a substance, such as spirit of vitriol, formed by distilling green vitriol. This caused more confusion than any other form of nomenclature since compounds which could be prepared in more that one way tended to have more than one name.

Towards the end of the eighteenth century advances in preparative chemistry led to the making of a large number of new compounds, and it became necessary to develop a fresh, less equivocal terminology. This was accomplished largely by Lavoisier, who decided to name the compound by the results of its analysis. The name of the compound would be made up of the elements which it contained, i.e. zinc sulphide contains zinc and sulphur. This was a classification based on the chemical characteristics of the compound and not on its physical characteristics.

In putting forward this terminology Lavoisier and his co-authors swept away all the alchemical associations between certain compounds and the heavens, or the deities, or anything else, and they concentrated on the facts. What did the compound contain? This was what interested the chemist, and so the name should reflect the analysis. In this way Lavoisier built up nearly the present system of nomenclature. Oxygen, which had recently been discovered, was considered to be specially important, and so the suffixes -ite or -ate were added if the compound also contained oxygen.

Linked to the history of chemical nomenclature is the history of chemical symbolism. The use of symbols as a kind of chemical shorthand is a very old practice. Abbreviations and pictograms were used both by the Greeks and the Egyptians. During the development of alchemy the use of symbols was widespread. As in the early nomenclature, alchemical symbolism took a number of forms. Some of them were mere abbreviations, some were pictograms, or symbolical signs, and some were merely arbitrary signs which grew up by convention to represent a certain substance. But one of the difficulties in interpreting alchemical symbols, as with all alchemical writings, is that in many cases the alchemists themselves did not want their own discoveries to be broadcast. Many of their symbols were a private shorthand which they did not want anyone else to be able to read, and which is therefore incomprehensible now. In their correspondence it was quite common for them either to write in code, and then send on the key to the code in another letter. Alternatively they might send on a riddle which included the problem, and send on the answer later. In this way only both halves of the manuscript would yield the alchemist's secret, so that if one half fell into the wrong hands it would not matter.

One of the most interesting things about the old symbols is that there were a number of attempts to produce compound symbols, which would represent a number of facts. However the compound symbols often included such information as the state of the compound, or its temperature, which tended to make them clumsy.

One of the first large-scale attempts to produce a symbolic notation came early in the eighteenth century. A chemist called Geoffroy thought of chemical reactions in terms of affinity. So he made out a table in which the affinities, i.e. reactivities, of a number of elements would be immediately obvious. It is shown in Plate 4.

On the top line are a variety of reagents. Underneath each one are the other substances in their order of affinities, those with the greatest affinity at the top, being able to displace substances beneath them. This table became something of a classic, and many other chemists tried to improve on it. It is important from

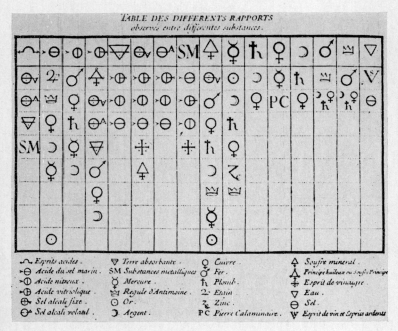

PLATE 4. Geoffroy's Table of Affinities.

our point of view as a system of symbols representing compounds, and, due to the success of the table, the symbols became well known.

Lavoisier, in his reform of nomenclature, also used some of Geoffroy's symbols, and a few more of his own. In the *Methode de Nomenclature Chimique*, published in 1787, after Lavoisier's explanation of the new nomenclature, comes the most ambitious of all the efforts to represent chemistry in terms of signs and symbols. Its authors were two young French chemists, Hassenfratz and Adet. They divided undecomposed substances into six classes, each with its own symbol.

1. Simple substances, commonly found
   as part of a compound   a straight line.
2. Alkalis and earths   a triangle.
3. Inflammable substances   a semi-circle.
4. Metals   a circle.
5. Acid radicals   a square.
6. Compounds whose constituents
   were not yet decomposed   a diamond shape.

They combined these simple substances into compounds, and by expressing their combination with caloric, they also showed their physical state. Two of their tables are shown in Plate 5.

Dalton used a much simpler system of symbols shown in Plate 6, but the great change which he made was to make his symbols represent single atoms. None of the previous symbols had been able to do this, of course, and none of them had been quantitative. They represented the elements qualitatively, and in order to make them quantitative they had to be preceded by the weight used in each case. This was a clumsy and tedious procedure.

Dalton's symbols suffered from two disadvantages. The first was that they could not be easily incorporated into a printed text; this disadvantage applied equally well to those of Hassenfratz and Adet. The second was that they suffered from being somewhat arbitrary, and although some elements were represented by the first letter of their name, others were represented by signs, which made memorizing them difficult.

Berzelius' symbols were closely associated with his work on atomic weights. He was greatly interested in minerology, coming from a country in which mining plays an important part in the economy. Dealing with complicated minerals meant that a shorthand would be desirable, so that he would not have to write out the full chemical formula each time. The first explanation of his new system was made in a British Journal, *Annals of Philosophy*, in

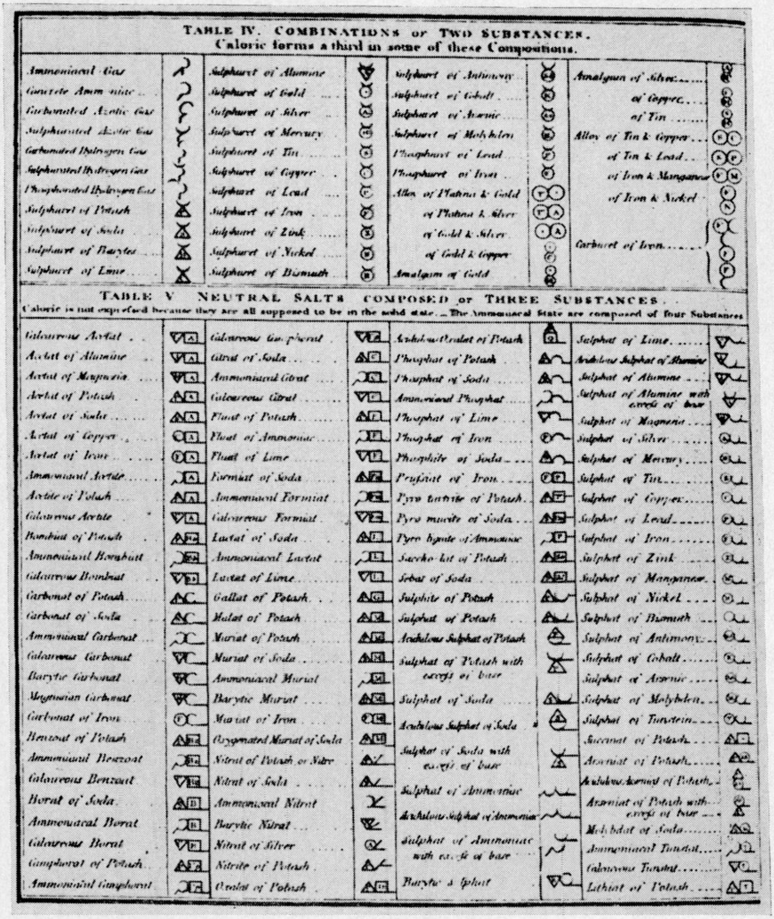

TABLE IV. COMBINATIONS OF TWO SUBSTANCES.
Caloric forms a third in some of these Compositions.

Ammoniacal Gas
Concrete Ammoniac
Carbonated Azotic Gas
Sulphurated Azotic Gas
Carbonated Hydrogen Gas
Sulphurated Hydrogen Gas
Phosphorated Hydrogen Gas
Sulphuret of Potash
Sulphuret of Soda
Sulphuret of Barytes
Sulphuret of Lime

Sulphuret of Alumine
Sulphuret of Gold
Sulphuret of Silver
Sulphuret of Mercury
Sulphuret of Tin
Sulphuret of Copper
Sulphuret of Lead
Sulphuret of Iron
Sulphuret of Zink
Sulphuret of Nickel
Sulphuret of Bismuth

Sulphuret of Antimony
Sulphuret of Cobalt
Sulphuret of Arsenic
Sulphuret of Molybden
Phosphuret of Lead
Phosphuret of Iron
Alloy of Platina & Gold
of Platina & Silver
of Gold & Silver
of Gold & Copper
Amalgam of Gold

Amalgam of Silver
of Copper
of Tin
Alloy of Tin & Copper
of Tin & Lead
of Iron & Manganese
of Iron & Nickel
Carburet of Iron

TABLE V. NEUTRAL SALTS COMPOSED OF THREE SUBSTANCES.
Caloric is not expressed because they are all supposed to be in the solid state. — The Ammoniacal State are composed of four Substances

Calcareous Acetat
Acetat of Alumine
Acetat of Magnesia
Acetat of Potash
Acetat of Soda
Acetat of Copper
Acetat of Iron
Ammoniacal Acetate
Acetite of Potash
Calcareous Acetite
Bombiat of Potash
Ammoniacal Bombiat
Calcareous Bombiat
Carbonat of Potash
Carbonat of Soda
Ammoniacal Carbonat
Calcareous Carbonat
Barytic Carbonat
Magnesian Carbonat
Carbonat of Iron
Benzoat of Potash
Ammoniacal Benzoat
Calcareous Benzoat
Borat of Soda
Ammoniacal Borat
Calcareous Borat
Camphorat of Potash
Ammoniacal Camphorat

Calcareous Camphorat
Citrat of Soda
Ammoniacal Citrat
Calcareous Citrat
Fluat of Potash
Fluat of Ammoniac
Fluat of Lime
Formiat of Soda
Ammoniacal Formiat
Calcareous Formiat
Lactat of Soda
Ammoniacal Lactat
Lactat of Lime
Gallat of Potash
Malat of Potash
Muriat of Potash
Muriat of Soda
Ammoniacal Muriat
Barytic Muriat
Muriat of Iron
Oxygenated Muriat of Soda
Nitrat of Potash or Nitre
Nitrat of Soda
Ammoniacal Nitrat
Barytic Nitrat
Nitrat of Silver
Nitrite of Potash
Oxalat of Potash

Acidulous Oxalat of Potash
Phosphat of Potash
Phosphat of Soda
Ammoniacal Phosphat
Phosphat of Lime
Phosphat of Iron
Phosphite of Soda
Prussiat of Iron
Pyro tartrite of Potash
Pyro mucite of Soda
Pyro lignite of Ammoniac
Saccho-lat of Potash
Sebat of Soda
Sulphite of Potash
Sulphat of Potash
Acidulous Sulphat of Potash
Sulphat of Potash with excess of base
Sulphat of Soda
Acidulous Sulphat of Soda
Sulphat of Soda with excess of base
Sulphat of Ammoniac
Acidulous Sulphat of Ammoniac
Sulphat of Ammoniac with excess of base
Barytic Sulphat

Sulphat of Lime
Acidulous Sulphat of Alumine
Sulphat of Alumine
Sulphat of Alumine with excess of base
Sulphat of Magnesia
Sulphat of Silver
Sulphat of Mercury
Sulphat of Tin
Sulphat of Copper
Sulphat of Lead
Sulphat of Iron
Sulphat of Zink
Sulphat of Manganese
Sulphat of Nickel
Sulphat of Bismuth
Sulphat of Antimony
Sulphat of Cobalt
Sulphat of Arsenic
Sulphat of Molybden
Sulphat of Tungstein
Succinat of Potash
Arseniat of Potash
Acidulous Arseniat of Potash
Arseniat of Potash with excess of base
Molybdat of Soda
Ammoniacal Tunstat
Calcareous Tunstat
Lithiat of Potash

PLATE 5. Tables showing Hassenfratz and Adet's symbols for various compound bodies.

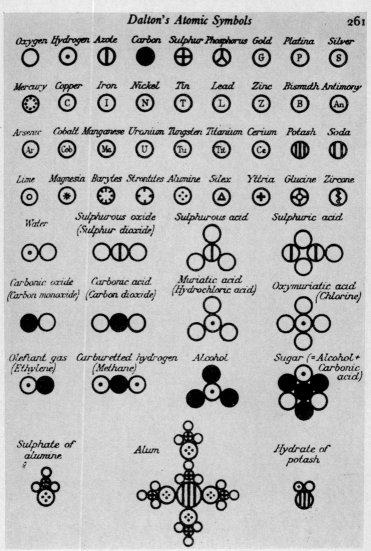

PLATE 6. Dalton's symbols.

1813. In it he says, "Let us express by the initial letters of the name of each substance a determinate quantity of that substance; and let us determine that quantity from its relation in weight to oxygen, both taken in the gaseous state, and in equal volumes; that is to say the specific gravity of the substances in their gaseous state, that of oxygen being considered as unity. . . .

"When two bodies have the same initial letter, I add the second letter, and should that also be the same, I add to the initial letter the first consonant of the word that differs. In the class of combustibles which I call metalloids, I shall use only the initial letters. . . . This is all that is necessary to understand these formulae. The only thing that remains to render the use of them more general is to determine correctly the specific gravity of the gases."

Berzelius' suggestion was soon adopted.

The important point in this system of notation is that the symbol for an element stands, not only to distinguish it from other elements, but also to represent a gram atom of the element. This quantity is much more useful that Dalton's atom, and it makes Berzelius' system capable of expressing chemical equations without the cumbersome addition of weights. Only Berzelius could do this because only he was confident of working out a system of atomic weights, as he says in the last sentence quoted.

Berzelius regularized the names of the elements by always using the initial letter of the Latin name for the element, as this was the international, and acceptable language. For simple compounds he used a plus sign between the elements,

e.g. $2H + O =$ water,

but for more complicated compounds he simply joined together the simpler components,

$$\text{copper sulphate} = CuO + SO^3$$
$$\text{alum} = 3(Al + 2SO^3) + (P + 2SO)$$

Berzelius wrote the exponent above the symbol, but this was later changed to its present position by Liebig. In later years Berzelius made some alterations to this system, mainly for the worse. To abbreviate formulae in minerology still further he had a special shorthand for common electronegative elements like sulphur, oxygen, selenium and tellurium. Because he overestimated the importance that two similar atoms played in a compound he also denoted two atoms of the same element in one molecule by writing the symbol with a bar through it. Both of these habits were dropped in later years. Also, for a long time Berzelius believed that chlorine and nitrogen contained oxygen, so that he wrote these elements as compounds of oxygen, a practice he later discarded.

It was largely due to Berzelius' great authority that the use of these symbols became common practice. Curiously enough the country which first heard of them, Britain, was one of the last to accept them. People spoke of these "abominable symbols" and even argued that writing CuO must mean that Cu was multiplied by O. Richard Phillips wrote that the language of symbols,

> . . . was a Babylonish dialect
> Which learned chemists much affect;
> It is a party-coloured dress
> Of parch'd and piebald languages;
> 'Tis English cut on Greek and Latin,
> Like fustian heretofore on satin;

but eventually they came to be accepted even here.

Chemical symbolism and nomenclature are the language of chemistry. The progress of any science is held up if the language is not clear and precise. The changes in the language of chemistry around the beginning of the nineteenth century reflected the changes in chemistry itself. The fact that a very great number of compounds was being prepared meant that nomenclature had to be made more systematic. What was required was a description of a compound that was both necessary and sufficient to describe its constituents. Berzelius said, "Permit me to remark that the purpose of these new symbols is not, as with the older ones, to serve as mere labels for bottles in laboratories. Their sole purpose is to facilitate the expression of combining proportions, and without undue verbosity to indicate the proportionate number of molecules in any given compound. In determining molecular weights these formulae will enable us to express summary results of any analysis that are as simple and easy to remember as the algebraic formulae used in mechanics."

OTHER WORK OF BERZELIUS

We have space here to give only a brief account of the rest of Berzelius' work. This is not because it was unimportant, but because much of the other work for which he is remembered was concerned with practical improvements and discoveries, rather than theoretical conceptions. However, there was one other field in which Berzelius made important theoretical contributions. This was the field of organic chemistry.

The division of chemistry into organic and inorganic originally sprang from the classification of substances into animal, vegetable and mineral, which was common in seventeenth-century text-books. Lavoisier made the first real progress in this field, when he showed that organic bodies contain carbon, hydrogen, oxygen, and sometimes nitrogen, sulphur or phosphorus. Bergman, another Swedish chemist, suggested that organic chemistry should be classified separately from inorganic chemistry, and there was a widespread belief that inorganic compounds could be prepared from the elements, but that organic ones require a "vital force" in their preparation.

During his researches on atomic weights Berzelius turned his attention to organic compounds, and proved that they obeyed the law of multiple proportions, and therefore that they were made up of atoms. He did not know what order of compound atoms they were, but he suggested that they were probably ternary or quaternary compounds. This work really opened up the field of organic chemistry to researchers, as Berzelius had developed a standard method of analysing compounds. In the next thirty or forty years most of the best chemists in Europe concentrated on organic chemistry, and laid the foundations for its rapid development.

Berzelius believed that Dualism was as applicable to organic as to inorganic chemistry, and he therefore proposed what is known as the "older radical theory". This was that a number of atoms could form a "radical", and that this could combine with oxygen to form a stable compound. The "radical" was, of course, electro-positive, and therefore it could not contain oxygen. This meant that Berzelius had to divide up organic compounds into oxygen, and the rest of the elements, a division for which there was no experimental evidence. It was suggested that since the "radicals" were like metallic elements they might be able to exist inde-pendently, and chemists tried to prepare them. This, of course, was fruitless, but it did lead to the discovery, in 1832, by Leibig and Wöhler that a "radical" known as benzoyl, from benzoic acid, did remain unaltered through a number of different re-actions. Unfortunately the benzoyl radical contained oxygen.

This discovery, backed by detailed experimental results, was so convincing that even Berzelius himself endorsed it for a while. However, he soon saw that it conflicted with Dualism, and with the important position which he gave to oxygen. So he backed down, although he still supported a modified "radical theory", in which the radicals did not contain any oxygen. Nevertheless, the "radical theory" did give a big impetus to many researches, as it was the first reasonably consistent theory in organic chemistry.

In 1834 Dumas made the discovery which we have already mentioned, namely that chlorine could be substituted for the hydrogen in acetic acid, without a major change in the properties of the acid. This spelt death for Dualism. Berzelius fought a losing battle against Dumas' discovery until his death. He did not deny that the chlorine had replaced the hydrogen, but he suggested that the two halves of the molecule were "copulated" or "con-jugated" together thus

$$CH_3 \xrightarrow{Cl_2} CO_2H \to CCl_3 + COOH.$$

This theory had no experimental justification, and of course still did not explain why substitution had occurred without change of properties, but it is interesting to note that we think of the compound today as being made up of essentially two different parts, the CH_3 and the $COOH$, and Berzelius' views were resurrected by Frankland and Kolbe, around the time of Berzelius' death.

Berzelius' other work in organic chemistry is impressive. He recognized, and named, isomerism when he discovered racemic acid and realized that it had the same chemical constitution as tartaric acid, but had different physical properties. This was an astonishing discovery at that time, and confirmed the work of Liebig and Wöhler that silver cyanate had the same constitution as silver fulminate. Berzelius even suggested that the difference might be due to the different arrangement of the atoms in the isomeric compounds, but of course he could not prove it. As well as this he differentiated between isomerism, metamerism, and polymerism, and he correctly defined them all. He suggested that allotropy, a problem which puzzled chemists for many years, was merely the isomerism of the elements. He discovered, and named, catalysis, suggesting the contact theory of fermentation. All of these discoveries, like many of his theories, showed that Berzelius was aware of, and was tackling, problems which other chemists did not catch up with for another twenty or thirty years.

We have already noted some of the many improvements he made in inorganic chemistry. But just to emphasize the vast range of his work and ideas we should note that during his years of analysis he discovered and isolated thorium and selenium, he isolated for the first time silicon, titanium, tantalum, and zirconium, and obtained the accurate atomic weights of about fifty elements. All of this was done in a converted kitchen, with equipment and raw materials he had to buy himself. This kitchen became the most famous laboratory in Europe, and served as a prototype for the more elaborate one at Geissen, run by Liebig. Berzelius' pupils included Mitserlich, Wöhler, and Gmelin, and while Berzelius was in Germany he met Goethe, and instructed him in the use of the blowpipe.

Berzelius reformed minerology as he had reformed chemistry. He set up a nomenclature which defined, rather than just described. This nomenclature was based on the chemical analysis of the minerals. At first it was based on the electropositive elements, but later he realized that it would be better to base it on the acid radicals, and this is essentially the system we use today.

CONCLUSION

We have tried here to give some idea of the prodigious achievements of this chemist. At a time when chemistry was a young and immature science, Berzelius tried to do the two things which were vitally necessary, to collect a number of accurate, reproducible, experimental facts, and to rationalize these facts into a system which gives them meaning and places them in perspective.

Berzelius seems to have lived a long and reasonable happy life. He was devoted to science, and little attracted to society life. Indeed he said, "I now feel more than ever before that an active scholar should never count on being or becoming a person who either gives or finds pleasure in social entertainment." He became very eminent, both in his own country and in the rest of Europe, but it does not seem to have made much difference to him.

He was happiest in the company of scientists. When he came to England in 1811, at a lunch in the Royal Society he found himself seated between Wollaston and Thomas Young, while opposite were Sir Joseph Banks and Sir William Herschel. He wrote afterwards, "This day, was one of the most memorable days in my life." In England he met Davy, and visited him. Davy had just married well, and had recently been made a baronet, so he seems to have been rather superior towards poor Berzelius. In Davy's writings Berzelius is described as "Indefatigable in labour, accurate in manipulation, no one has laboured with more profit. His manner was not distinguished, his appearance rather coarse, and his conversation limited to his own subjects." Berzelius certainly did not envy Davy's luxurious surroundings, but he did admire the much better equipment which Davy had at his disposal.

In 1818 he visited France, and made the acquaintance of Berthollet, Laplace, Cuvier, Gay-Lussac, Thenard, Dulong, Chevreul, Aragot, Biot, and Ampere. He also went to Germany and Switzerland. Late in life, when he was 56, he married, and was made a Baron. In his declining years he was fairly prosperous, but not extravagant. Although rather a retiring individual he seems to have been a very good teacher, and to have been admired and respected by his friends and pupils.

It is impossible, and unnecessary, to give a succinct summing-up of Berzelius' career and achievements. He was thorough and painstaking in his work; precise in his observation and accurate in his conclusions. Yet with all this he had a breadth of vision and a capacity for generalizing which was unrivalled while he was alive. His insistence on quantitative methods and reliance on experiment was a model for all scientists who came after him.

SUGGESTIONS FOR FURTHER READING

CROSLAND, M. P., *Historical Studies in the Language of Chemistry*. Heinemann, 1962
HOLMBERG, A., *Bibliographie de J. J. Berzelius*. Stockholm, 1933.
PARTINGTON, J. R., *A History of Chemistry*, vol. IV. Macmillan, 1964.
SZABADUÁRY, F., *History of Analytical Chemistry*, Chap. VI. Pergamon, 1966.

CHAPTER 3

THOMAS YOUNG, 1773–1829

THOMAS YOUNG was born on 16 June 1773, at Milverton, a small village near Taunton, Somerset. He learnt to read "with considerable fluency" at the age of two, and before he was four had read the Bible twice through. Under the guidance of Josiah Jeffrey, the school usher, Young learnt at an early age to use a lathe and to construct a telescope. It was to Jeffrey that he owed his introduction to optical instruments including their construction. Parallel with his interest in optical instruments was his great interest in languages, and during his youth he acquired a good knowledge of many languages, including Greek, Latin, French, Italian, Hebrew, Arabic and Turkish, to name but a few. At an early age, therefore, he had laid the foundations of much of what later were to be his researches in optics and oriental languages.

In 1768 the School of Anatomy was opened in Great Windmill Street, London, by William Hunter. He was later joined by his brother John, destined to become one of the greatest anatomists of all time. When Young entered the school in 1792, John Hunter was teaching there, although William (who died in 1786) had been superseded by his nephew, Dr. William Baillie.

After staying a year at the School of Anatomy, Young continued his studies at St. Bartholemews Hospital. It was during his first year as a student at the hospital that he wrote his first paper on vision. His medical studies, however, did not completely absorb his attention, and he found ample time to exercise his literary interests, in the fashionable literary group of the friends of his uncle Dr. Richard Brocklesby. It was the early encouragement of his uncle that had made Young enter the medical profession. Dr. Brocklesby's literary circle, in which Young moved, included such distinguished men as Samuel Johnson, Edmund Burke and Sir Joshua Reynolds.

Young's first paper on vision was published in the *Philosophical Transactions of the Royal Society*, and in the following year, at the age of 21, he was elected a Fellow of the Royal Society. The immediate reaction to Young's paper will be discussed later. After a further short period of medical studies at Edinburgh, Young proceeded to Göttingen to complete his medical education. Young described his final medical examination in the following manner:

> I made no preparatory study, as is usual here, and also at Edinburgh not uncommon under the name of grinding. The examination lasted between four and five hours; the four examiners were seated round a table, well furnished with cakes, sweetmeats, and wine, which helped to pass the time agreeably; the questions were well calculated to sound the depth of a student's knowledge in practical physic, surgery, anatomy, chemistry, materia medica, and physiology; but the professors were not very severe in exacting accurate answers. Most of them were pleased to express their approbation of my replies.

We may well imagine that with Young's linguistic abilities, his Latin thesis *De Corporis Humani Viribus Conservatricibus* was above fault. After Young returned to England he found that because of the current regulations concerning the practice of medicine he would have to spend two consecutive years at the university before being entitled to practice in or within seven miles of London. After much deliberation, he decided that instead of returning to Edinburgh, he would choose Cambridge, and was accordingly admitted as a fellow commoner at Emmanuel College in March 1797. In December of that year, Young visited his uncle, Brocklesby, and tragically Brocklesby died on the very night of Young's visit. Brocklesby left to his nephew his fine house in Norfolk Street, Park Lane, including the furniture, library, paintings (often selected by his friend Sir Joshua Reynolds) and about ten thousand pounds. After completing his residency at Cambridge (six terms) Young submitted to the Royal Society for publication what was to be one of his most important papers in the field of physical optics, entitled "Outlines of experiments and enquiries respecting sound and light".

With a background of London, Edinburgh, Göttingen and Cambridge, Young set up his medical practice at Welbeck Street, London, in 1799. Young had been in practice only a short time, when he was offered the Professorship of Natural Philosophy at the Royal Institution. His accepted the appointment. Apart from his lectures at the Institution, Young also edited its journal. His lectures, published in 1807 as *A Course of Lectures on Natural Philosophy and the Mechanical Arts* (2 volumes), have been described by Sir Joseph Larmor as "the greatest and most original of all general lecture courses".

OPTICS: INTRODUCTION

It had been considered since very early times, that light travels in perfectly straight lines, and that many facts could be explained by supposing light to be corpuscular. If we consider, for example, mirror reflections, the rectilinear propagation principle is affirmed. The whole science of catoptrics was built up on the early propagation theories of Euclid, Ptolemy, and later endorsed by Alhazen. The corpuscular or particulate theory of light remained virtually unopposed until the beginning of the seventeenth century, commencing with the speculations on the subject by Robert Hooke.

Just after the middle of the seventeenth century, examination of the shadows cast by a hair, by Franciscus Grimaldi (1613–63), showed that the fringes or stripes appeared within and also outside the shadow. Grimaldi's ideas that light might be of a wave nature were in many ways supported by Descartes, Huygens, Newton and Euler.

The following factors must be considered in attempting to explain the corpuscular and wave theories: (1) the rectilinear propagation of light; (2) the laws of reflection; (3) refraction; (4) simultaneous reflection and refraction at an interface; (5) the colours of thin films or plates; (6) diffraction; (7) double refraction. We shall briefly consider these points in turn.

Whereas a stream of corpuscles might be expected to cast sharp shadows, and not bend round corners, waves would not, obviously, appear to do this, e.g. sound waves are not entirely obstructed by objects, and the emitting sound source does not necessarily need to be seen to be heard. With respect to the laws of reflection, it may be said that neither theory exclusively explains that the angles of incidence and reflection are equal.

From the early considerations of Ptolemy (178–100 B.C.) it had been noted that a ray of light falling on a water surface was bent at the interface. It was left to Thomas Harriott (1560–1621), Willebrod Snell (1591–1626), and René Descartes (1596–1650), however, to establish a relationship between the angles of incidence and refraction, now known as Snell's Law. To explain this by the corpuscular theory it was assumed that the velocity of light in the denser medium was greater than in air. If the velocity of light in water was assumed to be slower than in air, then Huygens could show how Snell's Law was easily explained by the wave theory. At that time, however, no measurement of the relative velocities was possible (Römer verified the speed of light in 1675), and a decisive answer on this point had to wait until the "crucial" experiments of Fizeau (1849) and Foucault (1850).

Newton, in support of the corpuscular theory, explained the phenomenon of simultaneous reflection and refraction at an interface, by assuming that when the corpuscles reached the surface, some were in a state of "easy reflection" and some in a state of "easy refraction".

Robert Hooke in his *Micrographia* (1665) was one of the first to consider the colours of thin films or plates. He examined the colours of soap bubbles and oil spilt onto water. He tried to explain this by considering that a portion of the light is reflected at the surface of the film, and some reflected at the second surface, which then re-emerges to reinforce the first reflection, and that this reinforced reflection produces the sensation of colour on the retina.

Grimaldi had shown that the edges of a shadow cast by an obstacle were not in fact sharp, but consisted of a succession of narrow coloured bands, which followed the outline of the obstacle. Thus it appeared that the edge of the obstacle "interfered" with the rectilinear path of either the corpuscles or waves.

As early as 1669 Bartholinus had described the double refracting properties of Iceland spar (calcite), the subject being further elaborated twenty years later by Huygens. They showed that if a ray of light falls on the face of the crystal Iceland spar, there may be under some circumstances two refracted rays, one obeying the ordinary laws of refraction, and the other one, called the "extraordinary" ray, not obeying these laws. Huygens produced experimental evidence, much in favour of the wave theory, to explain this.

Newton, in surveying the foregoing evidence, although not entirely satisfied with the corpuscular theory (he introduced ideas of wave theory to explain Newton's rings) lent his authority and reputation to it.

We may now pass on to Thomas Young, who, with the possible exception of Euler, was the first serious challenger of the Newtonian theory, and whose work on the wave theory of light was his greatest contribution to theoretical physics. In a paper published in 1800 ("Respecting Sound and Light", mentioned above) Young raised some objections to the complete acceptance of the Newtonian theory, and the following year set out his ideas on the nature of light as follows:

Light is probably the undulation of an elastic medium,

A. Because its velocity in the same medium is always equal.

B. Because all refractions are attended with a partial reflection.

C. Because there is no reason to expect that such a vibration should diverge equally in all directions, and because it is probable that it does diverge in a small degree in every direction.

D. Because the dispersion of differently coloured rays is no more incompatible with this system than with the common opinion, which only assigns for it the nominal cause of different effective attractions.

E. Because refraction and reflection in general are equally explainable on both suppositions.

F. Because inflection is as well, and, it may be added, even much better explained by this theory.

G. Because all the phenomena of the colours of thin plates, which are in reality totally unintelligible on the common hypothesis, admit a very complete and simple explanation of this supposition. The analogy, which is here superficially indicated, will probably soon be made public more in detail; and will also be extended to the colours of thick plates and to the fringes produced by inflection, affording, from Newton's own elaborate experiments, a most convincing argument in favour of this system.

Young's first Bakerian Lecture was delivered in November 1801. He paid lavish tribute to the previous work of Newton and Euler, and propounded his wave theory of light. Young's four opening hypotheses are worth noting:

1. A luminous ether pervades the Universe, rare and elastic in a high degree.

2. Undulations are excited in this Ether whenever a Body becomes luminous.

3. The Sensation of different Colours depends on the different frequency of Vibrations excited by Light in the Retina.

4. All material Bodies are to be considered, with respect to the Phenomena of Light, as consisting of Particles so remote from each other, as to allow the ethereal Medium to pervade them with perfect freedom, and either to retain it in a state of greater density and of equal elasticity, or to constitute, together with the Medium, an Aggregate, which may be considered as denser, but not more elastic.

The various phenomena previously mentioned were then accounted for by means of the wave theory, and most important of all, Young explained the principle of interference, when two waves moving in the same direction can combine to either reinforce, partially reinforce, or extinguish each other. When the crests of the waves coincide, there will be complete reinforcement, and where crests of one set coincide with the troughs of the other, the effect will be that they cancel each other out. Extending this hypothesis, Young sought to explain the colours of striated surfaces, such as insect wing, mother-of-pearl, etc., by stating that the light waves from the minute scratches interfered with each other, and that as white light is constituted of various different colours, then the different wavelengths would interfere when the reflections were at varying angles, giving different path differences, and thus in some directions one or more colours would be reflected more strongly than in others.

NEWTON'S RINGS

When a spherical lens is placed on a plane glass surface, the exact thickness of the air film bounded by the two surfaces can be calculated at various points from the centre of the spherical surface. If the radius and various distances are known, the thickness of the air films will be the corresponding sagittae. If light then falls normally, and observation made along the path of the light, then "Newton's rings" will be observed. If the light is white, then the rings will have various colours, depending upon the path differences, which in turn depend on the thickness of the air film. Where the light is monochromatic, i.e. of one wavelength only, then alternate light and dark rings will be seen, depending on whether the path difference is one whole wavelength, or one half a wavelength, at that particular point. Young gave a successful explanation for the fact that at the centre of "Newton's rings" where the spherical surface and plate are in contact, and therefore the film of air practically of no thickness, there is darkness, where one would have expected reinforcement, as the path difference is nil. Young postulated that the two reflections take place under different conditions, one being from a dense to a less dense medium, and the other from a less dense to a denser one. In the second case, there is a phase change of half a wavelength, and thus, although there is no path difference, there is destructive interference. Young predicted that if the conditions of the reflections were reversed for the second reflection (i.e. both reflections occurring under the same conditions, all reflections going from a less dense to a more dense medium) then the centre spot would be light. He used a lens of crown glass, a prism of flint glass, and between them a layer of sassafras oil, and observed that what he had predicted was in fact true, the centre spot was bright, and the first surrounding ring dark.

Young's 1803 Bakerian Lecture to the Royal Society was published in the *Philosophical Transactions* the following year. The paper, entitled "Experiments and Calculations relative to Physical Optics", sets out details of one of Young's important and convincing demonstrations of the principle of interference. Young calculated the wavelength of light, and on comparing these results with those of Newton, and his own values, calculated from the colours of thin plates, Young was certain that light was transmitted by wave form motion.

Just at this point in the development of the wave theory, Young was subjected to a sharp attack and severe criticism in the *Edinburgh Review*. The author of these attacks was Henry Brougham (1778–1868), later Lord Chancellor. Young had criticized a mathematical paper of Brougham's at an earlier date. Although Brougham was ill-informed, and largely unqualified to criticize, the attacks carried conviction, thus delaying acceptance of the wave theory for some considerable time. Although Young's defence ("Reply to the animadversions of the Edinburgh reviewer on some papers published in the *Philosophical Transactions*") setting out the details of his experiments and even inviting Brougham to carry them out himself, the reply had virtually no circulation, and certainly did not succeed in counteracting the original damage. Young's reputation suffered accordingly, and as a consequence he had some difficulty initially in finding a publisher for his *Course of Lectures on Natural Philosophy and the Mechanical Arts*. Ultimately he did find a publisher, who agreed to pay him £1000 for his work (a handsome sum in those days); the two volumes were published, but Young never succeeded in obtaining the agreed sum of money.

We may now return to Young's optical researches. In one of his experiments he demonstrated that in order to obtain interference the two portions of light must be coherent, i.e. having the same phase distribution, and must travel in practically the same direction. Young found two very small holes or slits most suitable to show the interference fringes, and he calculated the wavelengths of red and violet light. His results agreed with accepted values.

It was not until 1816, when the Frenchman Auguste Fresnel (1788–1827) published his work in the *Annals de Chimie*, that Young received any substantial support for his theory. Even

W. H. Wollaston, while admiring Young's Bakerian Lecture, could not wholly accept the wave theory at that time. As a result of certain careful experiments, Wollaston published in 1802 a very guarded acceptance of the fact that some phenomena could be explained on the basis of the Huygenian theory.

An important obstruction to the acceptance of the wave theory was Laplace's memoir on Extraordinary Refraction, published in 1809. Laplace deduced the laws of double refraction by means of the corpuscular theory, and such was his reputation and influence that his opinion counted for a great deal in this matter. Young replied in the *Quarterly Review* (1809) contradicting Laplace's contention, and maintaining Huygen's theory that the double refraction was due to light travelling in the crystal in different directions with different velocities. He made an analogy with the case of sound travelling in wood along and against the grain. Young was also disturbed by the discovery of E. L. Malus (1775–1812) in 1809 that light reflected from a glass surface at a certain angle would be polarized. In Young's opinion the degree of value in a theory was in direct proportion to the usefulness of that theory to permit understanding of known facts, and in the co-ordination of these known facts. This much can be gathered from his article in the *Encyclopaedia Britannica* (1817) on Chromatics, wherein he tries to summarize the existing controversy. The article, of course, was a general statement of existing opinion, and Young came to no actual conclusion. He was, however, some-what perplexed by certain aspects of polarization. Some polarization phenomena were explainable by the wave theory, but sometimes anomalous results occurred. The great stumbling block to the progress of the wave theory at this time was the idea, drawn from the analogy with sound waves, that the light waves, if they indeed existed, were longitudinal. Young did in 1817 consider that there might be some transverse component, but even he did not then consider the possibility of the waves being wholly transverse. And when he did come to see that polarization was explicable by means of the transverse waves, he still considered that these were derived from the longitudinal ones!

At about this time Young became aware of the work of Fresnel, who must, together with Young, share the credit for the firm establishment of the wave theory. Fresnel had worked not only independently of Young, but also without any knowledge of Young's work. It was not until 1815 that Arago introduced Fresnel to the published work of Young. The following year Fresnel wrote in a most modest and humble vein to Young, and enclosed a copy of his paper. Arago also sent copies of papers by Fresnel, to Young. In the same year Arago, accompanied by the chemist Gay-Lussac, visited Young at his home in Worthing. A second visit was expected, but did not materialize, and in a letter to Arago, Young pays a somewhat lukewarm tribute to Fresnel, but will not allow that Fresnel could be considered as having discovered anything really new. Young's attitude was more or less that Fresnel had confirmed Young's findings, rather than having contributed any original work. This seems rather unfair, considering that Arago had pointed out to Young that Fresnel's work was done quite independent of any knowledge of Young's publications. In a letter to his friend, Hudson Gurney, Young credited Fresnel with the extension and application of his (Young's) theory of light. As will be seen later, Fresnel would not accept a subordinate role in this matter. The correspondence between Young and Fresnel is especially interesting as it serves to illustrate the way in which French scientific progress was "played down" in England, and vice versa. Fresnel had to fight for recognition in France also, and in a letter to Young in 1823 he complained that he was finding difficulty in becoming a member of the Académie des Sciences. Young, the following year, asked Fresnel to write an article on "Light", for the *Encyclopaedia Britannica*, and this was accepted by Fresnel, in spite of ill health which was beginning to make work very difficult for him. Fresnel complained to Young in some considerable detail, of the neglect that his work had received in England, and while yielding priority to Young, pointed out that he made the same discoveries independently, if later. This may be illustrated in the matter of the interference of polarized light. Young was admittedly the first to demonstrate the colours, but it remained for Fresnel to show that the incident light must be polarized, and that the emergent light must pass through a polarizer if interference is to produce colours. Fresnel was responsible too for the one link in the chain needed to complete the wave theory, namely, the demonstration that light waves were of transverse components only, and not longitudinal. As mentioned above, Young had considered the possibility of transverse waves, but was blinded by the analogy with sound waves, and thus still considered that longitudinal waves must play some part. Fresnel saw that the fact of non-interference of rays polarized in planes mutually perpendicular to each other was only explicable if light was a transverse waveform motion; and it was only timidity on the part of his co-experimenter, Arago, that allowed this fact to be published in Fresnel's name only. At last Fresnel received recognition from his British counterparts, when in 1825 he was elected a member of the Royal Society, and two years later was awarded the Rumford Medal of the Society, for his work on polarization. The same year, Young became a member of the Paris Académie. Arago, when informing Young of his election, had the unpleasant task of announcing the death of Fresnel, at the age of 29. John F. W. Herschel, who eventually came to accept the wave theory, considered that the contributions of Young and Fresnel could not be separated but that each was responsible for the development in a different manner, Young by a more or less intuitive contemplation and suggestion, and Fresnel by a more systematic analysis and experimentation. From Young's correspondence, it is known that this verdict met with his approval.

THE ROSETTA STONE

The key to the secrets of ancient Egyptian civilization was held in a slab of black basalt rock 45 inches long by 28 inches wide, and just under a foot thick. The piece of stone known as the Rosetta Stone (see Plate 7), after the town near which it was found, now resides in the British Museum. It was discovered by some French

PLATE 7. The Rosetta Stone.

soldiers in 1799, and was eventually ceded to Britain. It arrived in England in 1802. On the stone, which is extensively damaged, are three sets of inscriptions, the first is in hieroglyphics, the second in an Egyptian running script (demotic*), and the third in Greek. Since the end of the fourth century all knowledge of hieroglyphics had been lost, and assuming that the three sets of writing were of the same subject matter, then the stone could possibly be used as a key to the interpretation of the Egyptian writing. Matters, however, were not to be so straightforward. The first translation of the Greek was made by the Rev. Stephen Watson in 1802, and he was subsequently followed by Porson and Heyne, who made suggestions for the missing portions. This gave a reasonable idea of the general subject matter; an edict of an assembly of the priests of all the Gods of Upper and Lower Egypt held at Memphis. Silvestre de Sacy, a French archaeologist, then endeavoured to interpret the middle inscription, and succeeded with some of the proper nouns, but failed to establish an alphabet. The Swedish classical scholar J. D. Åkerblad, also had some success, but mainly with proper nouns.

Young came on the scene in 1814, having previously given some indication of an interest in Egyptology, several years earlier. From his investigations, it became clear that the inscription was incomplete, and that on a statistical basis, the frequency of recurrence of proper names in the two scripts not being the same, then the hieroglyphics could not be a literal translation of the Greek, nor could they be the original of the Greek. The fact that experts had been trying to break the code for the previous twelve years, with little success, did not daunt Young. Quite the opposite, as is apparent from his letter to Gurney, where he remarks that he is amazed that such little progress should have been made so far! He evinced interest in the work of Åkerblad and de Sacy, and was anxious to know what had prevented further publications from them. Considering the fact that they both had had twelve years start on him, Young concluded that Åkerblad had failed in

* Demotic or enchorial, refers to the native or simplified form of ancient Egyptian script.

his attempt. In a communication to de Sacy in 1814, Young questioned the use of Åkerblad's alphabet in deciphering other than the proper nouns. It should be noted that both Åkerblad and de Sacy had considered that the enchorial or demotic script was in fact alphabetical in nature. De Sacy replied that Åkerblad was reluctant to publicize his results, and that he was doubtful of the correctness of the alphabet that Åkerblad had derived. De Sacy, in passing, mentions for the first time Young's great rival-to-be, Champollion le Jeune, who apart from publishing a two-volume work on ancient Egyptian geography, also claimed to have deciphered the script.

After only a few months work, Young had effected a "translation" of the demotic script with corresponding known words in the Greek portion of the stone. He compared his results with those of Åkerblad, and found that there was an attempt to associate certain words in the demotic script with corresponding known words in the Greek portion of the stone. Young also found that there was a measure of agreement, but that he had in fact progressed beyond the stages reached by both de Sacy and Åkerblad. Young had observed that some of the demotic characters bore a resemblance to the hieroglyphics, and reached the important conclusion that the demotic script was derived from the hieroglyphics. This implied a symbolic significance to the demotic characters, and that therefore might possibly be not entirely alphabetical. Young then proceeded to obtain evidence which would support this idea. He studied all the inscriptions he could lay his hands on, even recruiting the Consul-General in Egypt to make available to him any likely material which came his way.

A considerable amount of new material had been made available in the *Description de l'Égypte*, which included reproductions of inscriptions on temples and of the funeral rolls. Young's progress was somewhat retarded by the poor quality of the reproduction. However, he found the subject matter of the funeral rolls and temple inscriptions to be of very little help. The last of the series of the *Description de l'Égypte* contained reproductions of a much better quality than the preceding numbers. Of these we find an example of a funeral roll named by Young the Codex Ritualis. It contained drawings appertaining to the journey of the deceased through the underworld together with the various prayers, etc. After noticing that many of the rolls appeared to have some sections which corresponded with each other, he was able to say with some certainty that the characters could not possibly have an alphabetical significance. He communicated this discovery to the Archduke John of Austria.

> I had already ascertained, as I have mentioned in one of my letters to Mr. de Sacy, that the enchorial inscription of Rosetta contained a number of individual characters, resembling the corresponding hieroglyphics, and I was not disposed to place any great reliance on the alphabetical interpretation of any considerable part of the inscription. I have now fully demonstrated the hieroglyphical origin of the running hand, in which the manuscripts on papyrus, found with the mummies, are commonly written, and which is obviously of the same kind with the enchorial characters of the Stone of Rosetta, as Mr. Åkerblad, and his disciple Mr. Champollion, have both justly observed. In the great *Description de l'Égypte* there are several engravings of manuscripts on papyrus; one of them contains more than five hundred columns of well delineated hieroglyphics, consisting, according to Mr. Jomard, of about thirty thousand characters, arranged under a series of vignettes, which run along the greater part of the margin. I was first struck with the evident relation of some of the figures in the margin to the text below; and having observed the same figures in the margins of several other manuscripts written in the running hand, I was led to examine with attention the corresponding texts and I found at last a similar agreement in almost all of them. I then made copies of the respective passages in continuous lines, and I found that the characters agreed throughout with each other, in such a manner as completely to put an end to the idea of the alphabetical nature of any of them. In this manner I obtained a duplicate, and sometimes a triplicate and quadruplicate copy of almost half of the great hieroglyphical manuscript, although not without some variation in particular passages: and in a manuscript of which Denon, if I mistake not, has published the first column, and of which an engraving has been obligingly sent me by Mr de Sacy, I have identified a few other passages of the great hieroglyphic manuscript, not found in either of the others contained in the *Description de l'Égypte*.

Young's hope was that he would be able to translate the demotic script back into the hieroglyphic form, as he felt that the demotic was a degraded form of the true hieroglyphics.

Of the three inscriptions the one which had suffered the most damage was the first. This had resisted interpretation even more strongly than had the running script, and there was very little for Young to go on. Young had decided that the group of characters enclosed in a ring or cartouche signified a proper noun. He was not the first to have this idea, as it had occurred to both Barthelmy and Zoega, neither of whom had been able to progress any further. Young could not possibly have known of this, and hence claimed this discovery as his own. He further concluded, using perhaps the analogy with Chinese, that the hieroglyphic script was ideographic, but that some of the ideograms might have phonetic values, and that also, if a conquerer's name was written

PLATE 8. Hieroglyphical inscription of the name Ptolemy enclosed by a cartouche or ring.

by his scribes in the language of a subjected country, then that name, if written in pictorial characters, would use the phonetic values of some of the pictorial characters. As in his previous conjecture, Young was not the first with this idea, but again it does not seem possible that he was aware of this, and using the aforementioned reasoning he was able to decipher the name of Ptolemy. Some of the hieroglyphs which he was able to identify are shown in the diagram (Plate 8), and illustrate the way in which he could put the letters together to form the word Ptolemaios (Ptolemy).

Young then attempted to apply his system of interpretation to another proper noun enclosed in a cartouche which he thought to be the name of Queen Berenice, and he came very near the correct result. Out of the thirteen signs contained in the two names, Young was entirely correct in six cases, partially correct in three cases, and wrong only four times. At a later date Young also added several more letters to the previous thirteen. Some of the cartouches, longer than the rest, appeared to contain the name Ptolemy together with some titles, and these Young found to be hieroglyphics denoting the titles of "Beloved of Ptah", and "Ever-living".

When we realize that the whole subject was a sideline to Young's other work, his article on Egypt, in the *Encyclopædia Britannica* can be considered monumental. The article published in 1819, and written a year earlier, was a comprehensive survey of the existing state of knowledge of the subject, the first example of its kind in English. It was divided into eight sections, and sections six and seven contain Young's original work. If we bear in mind that the article was anonymous, the following cannot be read without some amusement:

> a monument which has already enabled us to obtain a general idea of the nature and subject of any given hieroglyphical inscription, by pursuing the investigations already carried to an unexpected extent by an anonymous author, whose interpretation was communicated to the Antiquarian Society by Mr. Rouse Boughton . . . Mr. de Sacy, and more especially Mr. Akerblad, had made some progress in identifying the sense of the several parts of the second inscription of the stone; but it was left to British industry to convert to permanent profit a monument, which had before been a useless, though a glorious trophy of British valour.

The second section of the stone, the enchorial or demotic script, had developed from the hieroglyphics in about three stages, and bore roughly the same relationship to the hieroglyphics as does our ordinary hand writing to printed text. The development is a logical one paralleled by a similar development of the language from a formal "classical" to everyday usage. In evaluating Young's contribution to this subject, Peacock is of the opinion that a true judgement is impossible without reference to the original material on which Young had to work.

In his official capacity of foreign secretary of the Royal Society, Young received from Champollion a gift of the latter's two-volume work *L'Égypt sous les Pharaons*. This was in the year 1814, and in a letter accompanying the work, Champollion asked for some help in discerning some characters from the copies of the Rosetta Stone to which he had access. Young made some direct comparisons with the original stone in the British Museum and was able to give Champollion some of the help he required. There followed some correspondence, and Young sent to Champollion's brother a copy of his memoir on the translation of the demotic script. At this stage, de Sacy in no uncertain terms warned Young that there was a danger in too free a communication of his progress in the translation, as he felt that it was likely that Champollion would claim the work as his own. De Sacy, at this time, seemed to have a poor opinion of his fellow countryman's integrity. Champollion had commenced work on the translation of the Rosetta Stone nine years before Young, but at the time that Young's investigations began, it would not appear that Champollion was in a position to claim any success. The controversy which was to arise, between Young and Champollion, was not over a question of ability, but purely over that of priority. By the time that Young had published his article in the *Encyclopædia Britannica* (1819), Champollion had published nothing in the way of translation. This was to come two years later, and in it he stated, among other things, that the demotic script was not alphabetic, and that the demotic characters were not of a phonetic nature, but were ideographic. This, of course, was in complete opposition to Young, who based his decipherment of the names of Ptolemy and Berenice on the fact that the signs represented sounds. Champollion also completely failed to acknowledge Young's priority in the discovery that the demotic was derived from the hieroglyphic.

Young met Champollion in Paris in 1822, and was lavish in his praise. It was quite understandable that Young should recognize in Champollion an expert who was devoting his whole life, from the age of fifteen, to the study of Egyptology. But Young had misplaced confidence that Champollion would accord him the recognition that was his due. Champollion in his famous "Lettre à M. Dacier", in 1822, reversed his opinions of the previous year, and in fact contradicted himself. In this letter, Champollion, without acknowledgement, included signs, already deciphered by Young, in an hieroglyphic alphabet. He also utilized, without acknowledgement, the work of W. J. Bankes and Young, in interpreting the name Cleopatra.

Up to this time, correspondence between Champollion and Young continued in a very friendly manner, and Champollion made many requests for items in exchange for those forwarded by himself. Champollion's letter to M. Dacier was reviewed in the first number of the *Quarterly Review* for 1823. Upon seeing the review, Champollion wrote to Young expressing his extreme displeasure, as the review had attributed the embryonic hieroglyphic alphabet to Åkerblad, and the discovery of the derivation of the demotic writing from the hieroglyphic, to de Sacy. An examination of the chronological details will show that Champollion's protest was unjust and that the review was correct in its assertions. In various items of correspondence, Champollion continued to assert his right to priority, and he positively refused to be regarded as one who extended Young's alphabet, rather than its originator. Champollion's *Précis du Systeme Hieroglyphic* (1824) indicated considerable progress in adding to the derived alphabet. Although de Sacy had passed on Young's work on the demotic text to Champollion, Champollion persisted in the claim that he arrived at his results without any knowledge of Young's work. It was no doubt Champollion's great reputation which was responsible for the support of Busen and Arago (Young's friend). Arago was also influenced by the fact that Young had, by using what Arago thought to be his (Young's) system, made some errors in interpretation. Young made some effort to convince Arago of the justice of his case, pointing out that where he had erred, he had not in fact relied on any "system". Arago, however, was not to be swayed, and he remained unconvinced even after Young's death. As late as 1828, Young visited Champollion in Paris, a meeting

D

at which, one feels, it would have been most interesting to have been present. Champollion received Young warmly, and in spite of the fact that Young broached the subject of the dispute over the priorities, continued to extend every courtesy and hospitality to Young. He showed Young over the wonderful collection of items of Egyptological interest of which he had charge, and made many notes freely available to Young. Considering the bitterness generated by the controversy, it would appear that Champollion's attitude could be considered a little strange, and perhaps inconsistent. More than anything, the attitude of Champollion would seem to have been one of sheer obstinacy in the face of incontrovertible evidence. The priorities belonged undoubtedly to Young, as Young had obtained a "key", certainly not at that time in the possession of Champollion. Realizing Young's versatility, and his many other activities at the time, all credit for the initial discoveries is due to him. For reasons best known to himself, Champollion refused to acknowledge any debt to Young, a refusal which seems unnecessary when one considers his eminence in his chosen field, no one doubting his tremendous ability, or denying the vast extent and value of his contributions to Egyptology.

PHYSIOLOGICAL OPTICS

It was a paper written in May 1793 which was responsible for the election of Young, at the age of 21, as a Fellow of the Royal Society. The memoir (his first one in the field of optics) put forward Young's view that there was evidence to suppose that the fibres of the lens of an ox eye were of a muscular nature. He also discussed the means by which objects at different distances were brought to a sharp focus on the retina. Young postulated that the eye is in a relaxed state when focused for distant objects, and that an increase in the curvature of the crystalline lens is the means by which the sharp focusing of near objects is made possible (the mechanism of accommodation). It might be pointed out here, that this is generally agreed; it is the manner in which the curvature is altered that is the present-day problem. An important paper in the history of the physiology of the eye was that of Young's *On the Mechanism of the Eye*, published in 1801. Among other matters, it dealt with the optometer, the amplitude of accommodation, radius of curvature of the cornea, the axial length of the globe and his discovery of astigmatism. Theoretically, the measurement of the far and near points of the eye can be easily done with the Young Optometer, but from a practical consideration, several difficulties are encountered. The fact that an infinitely long base line is not possible (see Plate 9), is overcome by using a collimating optometer lens of known focal length. A graduated scale can then be used to show the various equivalent far and near points. The focusing action of the eye, however, is rarely at rest; in some refractive states it is more active than in others, and even then, the very "nearness" of the object being viewed can "induce" unwanted accommodation. These objections are still valid criticisms of many present-day optometers, although many ingenious methods have been adopted to overcome them. Taking the rather short distance of 8 inches for his normal near point, Young used an optometer lens of 4 inches focal length. The range of focusing, or "amplitude of accommodation" of the eye, is nowadays stated as a power rather than the focal length of a lens.* Young, however, specified the amplitude in terms of the focal length necessary to change the far point of the relaxed eye to its near point, and found the lens needed for his own eye to be of focal length 4 inches. The amplitude of accommodation diminishes from birth; it is as high as 15 dioptres in young children, and falls to virtually zero in the seventies.

Young proceeded to attempt measurement of some of the constants of the eye. In order to measure the axial length of his globe, he used a pair of compasses, to the points of which had been attached the rings of two keys, as a pair of calipers in the following remarkable manner: turning the eye inwards, he placed the ring on the sclera until the ring phosphene (i.e. the visual response evoked by pressure) caused by its pressure was central, and then

* The power in dioptres is the reciprocal of the focal length in metres.

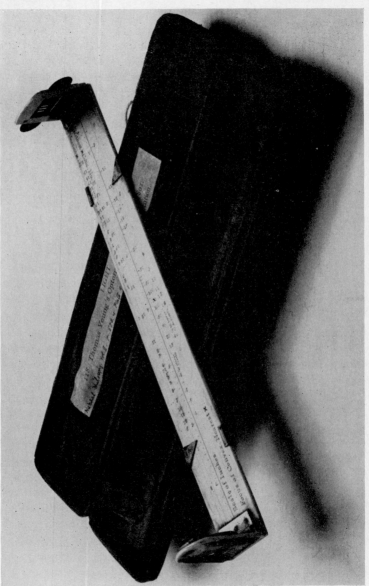

PLATE 9. Thomas Young's Optometer.

adjusted the other ring so as just to touch the apex of the cornea. Fortunately Young had rather protruding eyes, and with a greater amount of bravery than is possessed by most people, he was able to perform this type of experiment on his own eyes. In spite of the crudity of Young's methods, his result of 23 mm for the axial length comes well within the limiting values found by later workers, using considerably more refined techniques.

While carrying out further experiments with the optometer, Young made the discovery that his far point was different in two meridians, i.e. the phenomenon of astigmatism. In this condition the refractive power of the eye is different in two mutually perpendicular meridia, and is usually caused by a cornea which is not spherical in shape. This is not the only cause, and in fact Young's own astigmatism was probably due to a tilting of his crystalline lens. Young corrected the defect of his astigmatism by tilting his spectacle lens (or eyeglass) obliquely to its axis. The present day means of correcting astigmatism, by a cylindrical lens, was first shown by George Biddell Airy (Astronomer Royal, 1835–81) in 1824.

Other aberrations of the eye's optical system were investigated by Young, and oblique astigmatism, present even in a spherical system, was demonstrated and measured by him. The eye is not immune from some of the other aberrations common to optical systems generally. Spherical aberration, where the different zones of the lens have different focal lengths, can be positive where the peripheral zones have a shorter focal length, and therefore a higher power, or negative spherical aberration where the peripheral zones have a longer focal length, and a lower power than the central zones. Most, but not all, eyes suffer from positive spherical aberration, and Young found his own eyes had a little of this defect. The amount he found compares very closely with the average findings of later writers.

The power of a lens is dependent upon the radii of curvature of its surfaces, and the refractive index of the substance from which it is made. The refractive index of transparent media is different for various wavelengths of light, so that it can be appreciated that unless special steps are taken (and even if they are) an optical system, such as the eye, will refract rays of one colour more than those of another. The aberration is known as chromatic aberration. Young showed that the eye suffered from this defect and obtained an estimate of its magnitude. To enable the eye to focus near objects as well as distant ones (i.e. the phenomenon of accommodation) it is necessary for the total refractive power of the eye's optical system to increase, or for the axial length to increase, the net result being the same, i.e. rays diverging from a near object are focused sharply on the retina. This could be accomplished (a) by an actual increase in the axial length of the globe, (b) by an increase in corneal curvature, (c) by the crystalline lens moving forward, away from the retina, (d) by the crystalline lens altering its shape to give increased power, (e) by a combination of any of the foregoing. By a similar experiment to that in which he measured the length of his eye, Young showed that any in-increase in the axial length occurring whilst focusing a near object would result in an increase in the size of the phosphene. As no increase in the size occurred, Young concluded that the axial length of the globe did not increase during accommodation. The greater part by far of the total power of the eye is contributed by the anterior corneal surface. If this is almost neutralized by immersing it in a fluid of like refractive index (e.g. water) and then its power replaced by a glass lens, any possibility of its contributing to the focusing of near objects could be ascertained. In an experiment in which Young immersed his eye in water, he found no impairment of his powers of accommodation with his cornea thus neutralized. Incidentally, it was during this experiment that he also observed the continued existence of his astigmatism, showing that it was not due to his corneal anterior surface being toroidal. Young does not appear to have considered the forward movement of the crystalline lens as a contributory factor to accommodation. Modern work has shown that the lens does in fact move forward during the act of accommodation, but that this only gives a slight increase in effective power. Thus, Young was left with the hypothesis that the crystalline lens altered in shape. Jesse Ramsden and

Everard Home, in 1794 (following Young's early (1793) paper), maintained that the power of accommodation remained, even when the lens was removed. By experiments on numerous aphakic patients (i.e. patients whose crystalline lens has been removed), Young demonstrated that no power of accommodation existed where the crystalline lens was absent. He concluded that the alteration in the focal power of the eye must be caused by the crystalline lens altering in curvature, and although Young was erroneous in attributing this change in curvature to the "muscularity" of the lens fibres themselves, and not to a change in the cornea or axial length, in the important matter that accommodation is effected by an increase in power of the crystalline lens, he was basically correct.

COLOUR VISION AND COLOUR BLINDNESS

Newton had suggested that the different rays of light excited vibrations in the retinal terminations of the optic nerve, "the biggest, strongest, or most potent rays, the largest vibrations; and other shorter, according to their bigness, strength of power". These vibrations, he continued, "will run . . . through the optic nerves into the sensorium; and there, I suppose, affect the sense with various colours, according to their bigness and mixture. . . ."

After outlining and discussing Newton's theory of colour in detail, Young proceeded to state his own views as follows:

> . . . as it is almost impossible to conceive each sensitive point of the retina to contain an infinite number of particles, each capable of vibrating in perfect unison with every possible undulation, it becomes necessary to suppose the number limited, for instance, to the three principal colours, red, yellow and blue . . . and each sensitive filament of the nerve may consist of three portions, one for each principal colour.

The colours red, yellow and blue were later modified by Young, to red, green, and violet. He was, incidentally, aware of the apparent anomalies of colour mixing when using "pigments", as against mixing with "lights". In the first case, the mixing is of a subtractive nature, and in the second case an additive nature. In colour mixing experiments it is the additive method which is used.

Young suggested the use of the ancient idea of a colour top for some colour mixing experiments. This uses the phenomenon of the persistence of vision to mix the colours as the top is spun. Young modified Newton's colour circle, and his resultant colour triangle, in further modified form, is widely used by many workers in this field.

Young's theory was of course unsupported by any experimental evidence, but it had the merit of simplicity and gave an explanation of the facts of colour mixing and colour blindness deficiency.

It seems curious that with colour so obvious a part of everyday life, the phenomenon of colour deficiency went unrecorded for so long. Although there are one or two earlier cases in the literature, the most important early contribution to the subject was that of the famous chemist John Dalton (1766–1844). Dalton's paper describing his own and other cases of colour deficiency was presented to the Manchester Literary and Philosophical Society in 1794. Space does not permit a discussion of his interesting study. To Dalton, "All crimsons appear to me to consist chiefly of dark blue. . . . I have seen specimens of crimsons, claret and mud, which were very nearly alike. . . . Crimson has a grave appearance, being the reverse of every showy and splendid colour. . . . Blood appears to me red ; . . . it is not unlike that colour called bottle-green. . . ." Dalton believed that his vitreous humour was blue in colour, and thus absorbed red. Young's explanation of Dalton's case made use of his theory in supposing that the fibres necessary for the reception of red light were either defective in some way, or absent from Dalton's retina:

> He (Dalton) thinks it probable that the vitreous humour is of a deep blue tinge; but this has never been observed by anatomists, and it is much more simple to suppose the absence of a paralysis of those fibres of the retina, which are calculated to perceive red; this supposition explains all the phenomena, except that greens appear to become bluish when viewed by candlelight; but in this circumstance there is perhaps no great singularity.

Young's theory of colour vision was modified fifty years later by von Helmholtz, forming what is now known as the Young–Helmholtz trichromatic theory of colour vision. Although there are many and complex subdivisions of colour vision, Young's basic hypothesis is not contradicted, and it also holds its own against the numerous other theories which have been put forward since his time. Research into the mechanism of colour perception has made enormous strides, but recent advanced work has shown that, fundamentally, Young's theory is correct, and is borne out by experimental evidence.

ACKNOWLEDGEMENT

It is a pleasure to express my thanks to Alan G. Bergman, Esq., for his many helpful suggestions throughout the chapter.

REFERENCES

The list below contains the main works consulted. The author has leaned heavily on the writings of G. Peacock, and the more recent volume of A. Wood and F. Oldham. The work by the latter is particularly recommended to the reader who wishes to have a more detailed account of the topics discussed in the chapter, as well as a modern assessment of Young and his work.

PETTIGREW, T. J. *Medical Portrait Gallery* (London, 1840), vol. iv.

LARMOR, J., Thomas Young, *Nature*, cxxxiii (1934), 276.

PEACOCK, G., *Life of Thomas Young, M.D., F.R.S.* (London, 1855).

SCOTT BARR, E., Men and milestones in optics: Thomas Young, *Applied Optics*, ii (1963), 639–47.

WOOD, A. and Oldham, F., *Thomas Young, Natural Philosopher, 1773–1829*, (Cambridge, 1954).

YOUNG, THOMAS, *A Course of Lectures on Natural Philosophy and the Mechanical Arts*, (London, 1807), 2 vols. This includes his optical papers published in the *Philosophical Transactions*, cited in the chapter.

CHAPTER 4

L. J. M. DAGUERRE, 1789–1851
AND
W. H. FOX TALBOT, 1800–77

SEVERAL of the chemical and physical processes that are basic to photography were known well before the beginning of the nineteenth century. Yet until the early part of that century there is no record of any person producing permanent pictures by the agency of light. During 1839 L. J. M. Daguerre in France and W. H. Fox Talbot in England publicized the first practicable techniques for doing this: since that date their names have been closely associated with the invention of photography. The really important factor in their work is that they each discovered and published a means of *developing* a latent image, so that it became visible on paper or plate after a relatively short exposure to light.

The principle of producing images of objects in a *camera obscura* or dark box had been known for centuries. Such a device was described by the Neapolitan writer G. B. della Porta in the middle of the sixteenth century and its invention has often been attributed to him. However, Leonardo da Vinci had previously described a camera obscura and even before that it was known to Arabian philosophers of the eleventh century. Porta's camera obscura originally consisted of a darkened room with a small hole in one wall. When the sun was shining on objects outside the room, their image was projected on the inner wall opposite the hole. In fact the apparatus was a large pinhole camera with the observers inside it. Later, Porta used a convex lens to obtain a more satisfactory image. Following the suggestions of Porta, artists began using cameras to help them compose their pictures and to interpret three-dimensional scenes on two-dimensional paper or canvas. During the seventeenth century several writers made reference to portable forms of camera obscura, for instance Robert Boyle (1669) and Robert Hooke (1679). Various forms of these cameras were made, some with a mirror inclined at 45°, so that the image was formed on a horizontal screen much like a modern reflex camera. No special lenses were made for the purpose until the early nineteenth century, when W. H. Wollaston designed a meniscus lens.

At the beginning of the nineteenth century then, the camera had long been in use and the problem that faced artists of the time was how they might be able to fix the image they obtained by the action of light, without having to trace it on translucent paper. It was already known at that time, that light could alter the chemical or physical structure of a great many substances; Berzelius lists over a hundred in his *Textbook of Chemistry* (1808). In fact, the influence of light on silver nitrate was reported by an Italian physician named Angelo Sala back in 1614. Several workers in Britain, Europe and America started experimenting with these substances in the hope of obtaining permanent pictures. The first published work relevant to this problem was that of Thomas Wedgwood (1771–1805), son of the potter Josiah Wedgwood.

Wedgwood's work was reported by Sir Humphry Davy in the *Journal of the Royal Institution* during 1802, with some additions of Davy's own. Paper or white leather was soaked in silver nitrate solution then exposed to sunlight through a painting on glass held in close contact to it, as in a modern contact printing frame. After a considerable period of exposure a negative copy of the painting was produced. Similar results were obtained with leaves, showing the venation clearly; less successful effects were obtained with paper prints of engravings. Wedgwood did not succeed at all in his attempts to procure pictures with the camera, because its images were much too faint to have any noticeable effect on silver nitrate. Silver chloride was tried as a sensitising agent and was found to be superior but still too slow. Wedgwood's work really emphasized the two major difficulties that were encountered at that time; firstly, the incredibly long periods of exposure to light needed by the sensitive materials then known, and secondly, the problem of fixing the pictures once produced so that light no longer affected them and turned them completely black. Wedgwood's pictures had to be stored in a dark place and inspected by candlelight. Two important practical points were noted in the report; one, that blue light is far more effective in turning silver salts black than red light, the other, that the silver salts are more readily decomposed by light when impregnated on leather. Davy himself produced successful microphotographs by projecting images of small objects with a microscope in a darkened room, using the sun as a light source. It seems strange today that he did not try ammonia solution for fixing the images on silver chloride paper, since the property ammonia has of dissolving unchanged silver chloride after exposure to light had been recorded by the Swedish chemist Scheele in 1777. After the death of Wedgwood, Davy did no further recorded work in connection with photography, although he did report in 1814 that silver iodide is more sensitive to light than silver chloride.

As so often happens, the early work of the two Englishmen was forgotten for many years. Meanwhile, the Frenchman Nicéphore Nièpce earned the honour of being the very first to take a permanent picture from nature.

Joseph Nicéphore Nièpce (1765–1833) was the son of a King's Counsellor. He married in 1795. Most of his scientific work was in collaboration with his brother Claude (1763–1828). The family was rich and although much of their fortune had been lost during the Revolution, Nicéphore and his wife, together with Claude were able to return to their family estate near Châlon-sur Saône in 1801. There they succeeded in dispersing the rest of the family wealth on a curious invention called the "Pyréolophore" which propelled boats along the Saône; this was patented in 1807, but unfortunately never found any commercial use. The first photographic experiments of Nicéphore Nièpce were directed towards the photo-copying of engravings for further printing, a process he called "Heliography". He coated lithographic stones and later metal plates with a variety of light-sensitive substances, including varnishes that he had prepared himself. After exposure to the light he tried to etch the plates with acids. The engravings to be copied were soaked in oil to render them transparent and at first exposed to the sun in direct contact with the prepared surfaces, as were those of Wedgwood. In April 1816 Nicéphore Nièpce started to experiment with cameras and eventually succeeded in making negative pictures of views on paper sensitized with silver chloride. He does not appear to have found a satisfactory fixing process for these images, and, although according to his contemporary letters he tried to print positives of them, he was not successful. During 1816 Claude Nièpce moved to Paris to try to sell the "Pyréolophore" which still occupied much of the time of the two brothers.

In July 1822 Nicéphore Nièpce made a successful heliographic copy of an engraving, on a glass plate coated with bitumen. When the plate was exposed to sunlight through the engraving for about three hours the solubility of the bitumen in a petroleum extract was increased in the light parts of the picture. Thus the dark bitumen could be washed away from the parts of the plate that corresponded with the light parts of the engraving, while the parts of it that corresponded with the dark parts of the engraving remained coated. A positive copy of the original was made directly thereby, and it needed no further fixing process. This is in fact the basis of Nièpce's "asphalt" process of photography. The first picture has not survived unfortunately, but Nicéphore Nièpce continued along these lines with his experiments, making further copies of engravings on glass and on metal. In 1826 he made a photo-engraving that was successfully used as a printing block, by following the partial removal of the bitumen coating on a metal plate by petroleum extract with acid treatment.

The first permanent camera picture, which is still in existence today, was taken by Nicéphore Nièpce in 1826 using his "asphalt"

PLATE 10. World's first photograph.

process on a pewter plate. The exposure was inordinately long, about eight hours on a bright summer day, so that the shadow effects sought after nowadays to give "depth" to the picture were completely lost. The photograph is quite large—20·5 cm. × 16·5 cm—and is a direct positive, like the earlier copies of engravings. The invention of the iris diaphragm type of lens stop

PLATE 11. Earliest extant daguerreotype.

and the first use of a leather bellows in a camera have also been attributed to Nicéphore Nièpce during the years following his success of 1826. It was during the January of the same year that he first heard of the experiments of Daguerre.

The first practicable photographic process, the daguerreotype, takes its name from Louis Jacques Mande Daguerre (1789–1851). He was born at Cormeilles-en-Parisis on 18 November 1789, the son of a courtroom attendant. In 1790 the family moved to

Orleans where Daguerre's father became employed as an official on the Royal Estates. He could afford only to send the boy to the local *école publique* or elementary school at Orleans, where the standard of education does not seem to have been very high. However, Daguerre soon showed considerable artistic talent in addition to natural intelligence and initiative. He was apprenticed first to a local architect (1801) and later (1804) to the artist Degotti, the chief scene designer at the Paris Opera. With Degotti he received very useful training in lighting and stage effects. After about three years he became assistant to Pierre Prevost, famous in his day as a painter of panoramas—then a popular form of entertainment. During 1810 Daguerre married Louise Georgina Smith (or Arrowsmith, born 1790). He exhibited his first independent painting in public at the Paris salon in 1814. All his work was of the type nowadays rather disparagingly referred to as "photographic". He was a very skilful draughtsman and could portray nature most realistically. In 1816 Daguerre became chief designer at the Théâtre Ambigu-Comique in Paris. There his talents rapidly developed and he soon became famous for his startlingly realistic stage effects. In 1819 he was invited to become one of the designers at the Opera, where he had previously served an apprenticeship. Again Daguerre's work was very well received.

The Paris Diorama, an improved form of panorama, was opened by Daguerre in partnership with the artist C. M. Bouton in 1822. In the Diorama, by a clever arrangement of lighting, enormous paintings of views, interiors, etc., appeared to change before the eyes of the audience; night would give way to day, volcanoes would erupt, churches would fill with people. The paintings were made on thin linen and illuminated with different coloured lights from either or both sides to give the changing effects. There were three picture rooms in the Paris Diorama, usually one in preparation for a new painting and the audience were seated in a circular chamber which rotated to face each effect in turn. In 1823 Daguerre opened a second Diorama at Regent's Park in London. Contemporary accounts are filled with wonder at the realism of these ingenious devices. Soon Dioramas were opening in other cities, those in Britain and America showing the paintings of Daguerre and Bouton that had previously been seen in Paris and London; but those in some countries showing the work of different artists. At first Daguerre and Bouton made money from the Dioramas, but after a few years the Paris one alone proved insufficient to support both of them and Bouton moved to London. There he became manager and artist to the Regent's Park Diorama.

Daguerre had given up his work on theatre scene designing before the Diorama opened in 1822. In 1824 he was made a Chevalier of the Legion of Honour in recognition of his paintings and his work at the Diorama. At about that time he first started making photographic experiments. He is certain to have used a camera obscura to help him with his work at the Prevosts' panorama and at the Diorama. Like many other people at this period, he became obsessed with the idea of making a permanent record of the beautiful but evanescent images he saw. In the course of his painting work he had encountered a variety of substances that became phosphorescent under the action of light. Daguerre used some of these materials in his early photographic experiments. Paper coated with silver chloride was also used by him as it was by Wedgwood and later Talbot in England, but Daguerre was unable to fix the images obtained. He obtained lenses for his cameras from the optician Charles Chevalier and the two men soon became friends, meeting to discuss the progress of Daguerre's work. This led to the meeting with Nicéphore Nièpce, for one day early in 1826 a cousin of the Niépces came to Chevalier's shop to order a new camera bringing with him one of their heliographic plates. It is believed that a few days after this event, which already had surprised Chevalier, a young and apparently poor man appeared in the shop with photographic prints of some sort on paper, and gave Chevalier a bottle of a light sensitive substance to try for himself. Neither Chevalier nor Daguerre could obtain any results with this substance, but the occurrence did lead Chevalier to tell Daguerre of the attempts of Nicéphore Nièpce, and to give him the address of the latter. Daguerre first wrote to Nièpce in the January of 1826.

The quiet and cultured Nièpce did not appear to like being approached directly by the self-made showman of the Diorama, and wrote a guarded reply a few days later, being very careful not to divulge anything of his process. Daguerre let the matter rest for over a year but increased his own researches so that he was rarely to be seen in public, spending most of his time in his laboratory at the Diorama building where he lived. Then, in February 1827, he wrote to Nièpce again, and received another cautious reply. In March Daguerre sent a drawing on glass to Nièpce, possibly in the hope that Nièpce would send him a heliographic engraving in return. Nièpce did in fact do this, in the June of the same year, but carefully removed all the bitumen coating from the pewter plate leaving only the lines etched by acid, so that Daguerre could still not deduce his process. However, the unfortunate circumstance of Claude Nièpce's illness in London during August 1867 caused Nicéphore Nièpce to travel with his wife to Paris on the way to London. While in Paris Nicéphore Nièpce met Daguerre in person, and visited the Diorama. He was evidently very favourably impressed with Daguerre's talents at the Diorama, and although Daguerre had no very impressive photographic results to show him, he seemed quite taken by the artist's cheerful, confident personality.

Claude Nièpce had gone to London in hope of selling the Pyréolophore. He was very ill when Nicéphore and his wife saw him and he died in February 1828, soon after their return to France. While in England they stayed at Kew from whence Nicéphor Nièpce tried to sell his invention of Heliography. He tried to interest King George IV through the help of the Director of the Royal Botanic Gardens at Kew, and the Royal Society through the botanist Francis Bauer, a fellow of the Society. As Nièpce was not prepared to give details of his process without first patenting it, no one was interested and he returned to France disappointed. He left in England several heliographs and prints from heliographs, also (with Francis Bauer) his first photograph from nature and a memoir on his process. The memoir contains the first suggestions of using polished silver plated metal for receiving heliographic images.

On the way home Nicéphore Nièpce and his wife again stayed in Paris where further meetings with Daguerre took place. In May 1828 Nièpce resumed his photographic experiments, now using a camera with a meniscus lens of the type designed by W. H. Wollaston and obtained from Chevalier. He stopped trying to copy engravings and concentrated on views from nature, but still with the idea of eventually producing printing plates. During 1829 Nièpce used iodine vapour to darken parts of his exposed bitumen and silver coated plates. When the bitumen was dissolved away completely a positive picture remained, the light parts being the unchanged polished silver and the shaded parts silver coated with silver iodide. Iodine was not used as an agent to sensitize the silver at this stage. Although Nièpce had succeeded in obtaining fixed pictures from his camera he was still troubled by the great length of exposure necessary. He thought the answer to this problem lay in the design of the camera and lens rather than in the improvement of his chemical techniques. The belief that Daguerre had an improved and rapidly acting camera led him to agree to join forces with Daguerre late in 1829, and form a partnership for the improvement and eventual exploitation of Heliography.

The contract signed by Daguerre and Nicéphore Nièpce in December 1829 was drawn up by a notary and lasted for ten years. Each partner was bound to tell the other all his findings relevant to the process and to keep them secret from outsiders. Each was to receive half of the profits from the sale of the invention. Most of the technical details were supplied in fact by Nièpce. Daguerre's improved camera did not have the expected effect in speeding the process but it certainly had an improved lens, the work of Chevalier, and was the first camera recorded to have been made of metal. It was to this camera that Nièpce first fitted an iris diaphragm. From 1829 to the death of Nièpce in 1833 the two partners worked separately, communicating frequently by letter, but never meeting again in person. Both worked with silver coated metal plates exposed to iodine fumes and thereby covered with silver iodide, now using the iodide as a light sensitive material. It is not certain which of the partners first tried this. They both experimented further with the "asphalt" process.

After the death of Nicéphore Nièpce in July 1833 his share of the partnership was inherited by his son Isidore Nièpce (1795–1868). Isidore Nièpce did not continue the work, so that all improvements to the process during the next six years were due to Daguerre alone. Daguerre tested a great variety of substances that he hoped would improve the image obtained on silvered plates. Although at first he continued to use bituminous preparations, he later concentrated his attention on plates coated with silver iodide. In addition to the problem of the very long exposure to light needed by these plates, they also had the disadvantage that they produced negative images. During the Spring of 1835 Daguerre found a solution to both these difficulties—treating the exposed plates with mercury vapour. He is believed to have discovered the effect of this at first sight rather unlikely substance accidently. There was a cupboard in Daguerre's workshop that contained a selection of apparatus and chemicals, including a few drops of mercury in a dish. One day he put into the cupboard some plates that had been exposed to light in a camera but had no visible images on them. The next day he opened the cupboard and found, to his surprise, that perfect positive images had appeared on the plates. Daguerre proceeded to make a series of similar plates, exposed them in the camera for a while, then put them in the cupboard and removed the chemicals one at a time until he found the substance responsible for the unexpected result. Whether this story is true or not, Daguerre did find what he had sought for so long. Henceforward a plate did not have to be left in the camera until an image had appeared as in all previous experiments; a latent image, formed during an exposure of half an hour or less, could now be "developed" by mercury vapour.

This very important discovery led Daguerre to insist on a revision of the original contract with Nicéphore Nièpce, making himself in effect the senior partner to Isidore Nièpce. At this stage Daguerre could still not *fix* the pictures obtained. A few months after this Daguerre was reported in an artists' periodical to have announced the discovery of his process, without giving any details, of course. As a result of this he met an amateur experimenter named Hubert who later became his assistant. Finally in 1837 Daguerre found that a strong solution of common salt could be used to remove unchanged silver iodide from his exposed and developed plates, thereby fixing them. A second revision of the contract was then made with Isidore Nièpce, in which the latter reluctantly agreed that the new process should be known under Daguerre's name alone, but that it should only be published in conjunction with the original process of Heliography. They then attempted to sell the two processes by public subscription.

The terms of the proposed subscription were that the processes would not be published until one hundred subscribers had been found, each prepared to put forward a thousand francs. The limit set to the number of subscribers was four hundred and the period of subscription was from 15 March 1838 to 15 August 1838. There was also a stipulation that the inventions could be sold to any one purchaser at a price not less than two hundred thousand francs. Daguerre did his best to find a purchaser before the subscription opened. Having failed to do so he tried to attract attention during the subscription period by driving around Paris with a cart loaded with photographic apparatus, taking pictures. In spite of this a sufficient number of subscribers was not forthcoming so he planned a second brief subscription scheme for January 1839, with printed broadsheets and an exhibition of actual daguerreotypes in addition to announcements in various newspapers. Daguerre also tried to obtain the support of a number of eminent scientists and artists before the second subscription scheme opened. The physicist and politician F. J. D. Arago (1786–1853) saw the value and importance of Daguerre's process. Realizing what restrictions would be imposed on its applications and subsequent improvement if it were to become a patented commercial process, he advised Daguerre to defer the subscription while he put a proposal to the French Government. This proposal was that the Government should purchase the process from Daguerre and Isidore Nièpce, and that it would then be published so that it was available for anyone to use. At a meeting of the Académie des Sciences in January 1839 Arago enthusiastically described the results obtained by Daguerre and outlined many possible uses. His speech was reported by the newspapers and soon claims of earlier inventions were put forward in France and other countries. Many of these claims were false, but one that could not be dismissed was that of Fox Talbot in England.

On 8 March 1839 the Paris Diorama building was destroyed by fire. As it was insufficiently insured Daguerre could not afford to rebuild it—previously it had been running at a loss anyway. Later on Daguerre's former partner Bouton built a new Diorama in Paris. Arago then increased his efforts towards encouraging the French Government to buy the Daguerreotype process. In August 1839 a bill was finally signed by King Louis-Phillipe giving an annual pension of six thousand francs to Daguerre and four thousand francs to Isidore Nièpce. Once this was passed Daguerre was obliged to publish details of Nièpce's work on Heliography. He also undertook to reveal his techniques used in painting the Dioramas, this gaining him the larger pension than Isidore Nièpce—really this was a manoeuvre by Arago who considered Daguerre to have made the larger contribution to the invention of the daguerreotype.

The details of the process were announced by Arago at a joint meeting of the Académie des Sciences and the Académie des Beaux-Arts on 19 August 1839. There was great excitement throughout Paris following the announcement. Large numbers of people rushed to buy cameras and materials to try the process for themselves. Meanwhile Daguerre had made a contract to supply cameras and equipment with the firm of Giroux, and a contract with Chevalier to supply lenses. Giroux also undertook to publish the first instructional manual on the daguerreotype. Daguerre received a share in the profits from the sales of these firms, but as the process was not patented many other firms soon began to copy and improve the apparatus. For several months Daguerre gave free demonstrations and advice on the new process at a number of public institutions in Paris.

In 1840 Daguerre retired to the village of Bry-sur-Marne just outside Paris. He had been made an Officer of the Legion of Honour in 1839. He built an extension to his house at Bry-sur-Marne containing a darkroom, a studio and a laboratory where he continued to take photographs by his own process. Although he had undertaken to publish any improvements he might make to the process he did not in fact discover anything new himself. He also continued to paint, and in 1842, using his earlier scene-painting techniques, painted a *"trompe-l'oeil"* picture behind the altar in Bry church. This made the church appear very much larger than it actually was. After an active retirement Daguerre died on 10 July 1851, and was buried two days later.

Although Nicéphore Nièpce had produced the first photograph ever taken from nature, and had been responsible for several of the ideas underlying the daguerreotype process, Daguerre had so perfected the process that it became suitable for anyone to use successfully after some practice. Its use spread rapidly in Europe and America. Only in England and Wales was it restricted, because there Daguerre had succeeded in obtaining a patent just before the process was announced in France. (This was not noticed, conveniently, by the French Government.) Some very fine photographs were produced from the earliest days of the daguerreotype, they had a fineness of detail and a good range of tones. The dark parts of the pictures were formed by bare polished silver, the lighter parts by mercury amalgam of varying density. They needed to be viewed at a particular angle to obtain the best effect. There were several disadvantages to Daguerre's process, some of which were overcome shortly after its publication. It was originally much too slow for portrait work. This was overcome by using bromine or chlorine to sensitize the plates, resulting in a more rapidly acting sensitive layer, and also by using larger lenses and smaller plates. The pictures were laterally inverted, but this could be corrected by using a reversing prism, as had been done in some old drawing cameras. The finished photographs were very easily damaged as the mercury layer was liable to be removed by the lightest rubbing. Gold toning of the plates made them more durable and also improved their appearance. Sometimes daguerreotypes were coloured by hand. One great disadvantage they had was that each one was unique. Several workers devised means for converting them into printing blocks but these processes were not suitable for general use. Daguerre himself did not approve of such devices for multiplying his pictures, which he liked to regard as individual works of art. From about 1850 stereoscopic daguerreotypes became popular. The process was practised until about 1860, when it gave way to the processes then available for producing negatives from which an unlimited supply of positive prints could be obtained.

The name of William Henry Fox Talbot (1800–77) has been associated with negative/positive photographic processes from the first. He was a grandson of the Earl of Ilchester and was born at Melbury in Dorset. His father died six months after he was born and his mother later remarried. Fox Talbot was educated at Harrow and Trinity College, Cambridge. At Cambridge he showed special interest in classics and mathematics. He was elected a member of the Royal Astronomical Society in 1822 and a Fellow of the Royal Society in 1831. In 1826 he went to live at the Talbot family estate, Lacock Abbey in Wiltshire. He married Constance Mundy, a clergyman's daughter, in 1832. For a short while, 1833 to 1834, Fox Talbot represented Chippenham in Parliament as a Liberal. He lived the life of a country squire at Lacock, devoting most of his time to his very varied scientific interests of which photography really formed quite a small part. He contributed papers to a great many scientific publications during his life, particularly on mathematical subjects.

Fox Talbot was very fond of foreign travel and like the majority of such travellers today wished to make a record of the scenes and

PLATE 12. View of Lacock Abbey.

buildings he saw for future reference. In October 1833 he visited Lake Como in Italy, where he tried using the camera lucida, an aid to drawing by means of a prism invented by W. H. Wollaston, but found he lacked the necessary skill. Next he tried tracing on translucent paper in a camera obscura, but still found the operation slow and tedious. Thus, on his return to England, he was led to start experimenting with light sensitive substances in the hope of causing rays of light to produce permanent pictures for him.

Even though he was not aware at this stage of the work of Wedgwood and Davy, Fox Talbot did know of the blackening of silver nitrate by light. He started by soaking paper in silver nitrate solution and exposing it to sunlight while held in close contact with pieces of lace or leaves. Finding, as Wedgwood had done, that the reaction of silver nitrate was too slow, Fox Talbot impregnated his paper with silver chloride by alternate washings in silver nitrate and sodium chloride (common salt). By this means he discovered the important point that his paper was much more sensitive to light if it contained an excess of silver nitrate. Moreover, he found later that an excess of sodium chloride retarded the action so much that a final washing in strong sodium chloride solution could be used to fix the pictures obtained after exposure. (Daguerre, it will be remembered, also used sodium chloride to fix his photographs.) Fox Talbot's first attempts to take pictures with a camera obscura were hindered by excessively long exposures. Like the improvers of the daguerreotype he then tried using smaller cameras; he produced paper negatives one inch square. With these cameras he obtained several views of Lacock Abbey, using exposures of about half an hour, during the summer of 1835. He also obtained successful photographs through a microscope.

For the next three years or so Fox Talbot made no further progress with his photographic experiments. Then, on 7 January 1839 Arago announced the discovery of the daguerreotype in France. This led Talbot immediately to send notes to Arago and the French physicist J. B. Biot claiming priority of invention, for he feared he would lose all credit for his work if Daguerre's method proved to be the same as his. By the end of January Fox Talbot had exhibited a selection of "Photogenic Drawings", as he called his pictures, at the Royal Institution and at the Royal Society. With the latter exhibition he presented a paper on his process, in which he described, for the first time, how he had obtained positive photographic pictures by contact copying of negative ones. There were copies of engravings produced in this way included in the exhibition.

Before the details of Daguerre's process were announced in August 1839 it had become apparent that Fox Talbot's process was not only different from that of the Frenchman but also inferior in the results. This did not deter several early speculators in England from preparing and advertising "Photogenic Drawing Paper" early in 1839. The first camera made to be sold specifically for photographic purposes was advertised in June of the same year.

Fox Talbot then set about trying to improve his process, buying new and improved cameras from the optician Andrew Ross. During 1840 Ross told him of the effect of gallic acid as an accelerator on the reaction of silver salts with light, a fact he had learned from the Reverend J. B. Reade. From subsequent experiments with gallic acid in connection with his process Talbot discovered the important principle of development of a latent image. He had made some apparently unsuccessful exposures in a camera with gallic acid activated photogenic paper, and began to sensitize the paper with a mixture of silver nitrate solution and more gallic acid. To Talbot's surprise the images he thought he had failed to obtain manifested themselves upon the paper. This, like Daguerre's earlier discovery of development of latent images on silvered plates with mercury, meant that camera exposure times could be shortened considerably. Fox Talbot informed Biot of his latest discovery and in January 1841 Biot read his statement to the French Académie des Sciences. During June Talbot described his work to the Royal Society in London.

In February 1841 Talbot patented his improved process in England and Wales. He called the process "Calotype". It was sometimes referred to afterwards as "Talbotype". Back in 1819 the astronomer Sir John Herschel, F.R.S., had discovered that sodium thiosulphate (photographers' "hypo") would dissolve silver salts. On 14 March 1839, in a paper read to the Royal Society, he drew attention to the application of this reaction in fixing photographs. Daguerre adopted the use of "hypo" as soon as he heard of it and incorporated it in his process as published in August 1839. Fox Talbot, however, continued to fix his productions with either sodium chloride or potassium bromide solutions, both of these being less efficient than sodium thiosulphate. Then, in a fresh patent of 1843, he included the use of this important substance in the calotype process as though it had been his own discovery. The progress of photography in Britain was unfortunately hampered for the next ten years or so by the patents of Fox Talbot. Britain was also the only country in which the daguerreotype was patented. Talbot patented every process he could partly in hope of gaining financially—although a land owner he was not rich—and partly so that his discoveries should be recognized. He quite rightly had come to expect no official recognition of his work in Britain as Daguerre had received in France, although he was given the Rumford Medal by the Royal Society for the calotype process in 1842.

As previously mentioned, gallic acid was used as an accelerator in photography by the Rev. J. B. Reade before Talbot heard of it. Joseph Bancroft Reade (1801–70) was born at Leeds and educated first at a local grammar school then at Trinity and Caius Colleges, Cambridge. He was ordained in 1826. Reade was one of those extremely keen amateur scientist clergymen that flourished in the nineteenth century. He was a founder member of the Microscopical Society and for a time its President. Like Fox Talbot he was a Fellow of the Royal Society and a member of the Astronomical Society. He used to find difficulty in drawing the objects he saw down his microscope, just like many students today. Familiar with the earlier work of Davy and Wedgwood,

114 EARLY NINETEENTH CENTURY EUROPEAN SCIENTISTS

he tried projecting microscope images on a screen in a darkened room then placing silver chloride coated paper on the screen. Reade noticed that Wedgwood and Davy had found silver salts were more easily decomposed by light when on leather, so he used some of his wife's old leather gloves and found a definite improvement. As the supply of leather from this source soon ran out, early in 1837 he tried "tanning" paper with an infusion of nut-galls (a natural source of gallic acid). When this "tanned" paper was treated with silver salts and exposed to light it rapidly turned black all over. Consequently Reade had to use a much more dilute solution of gallic acid. He found the most effective method was to first impregnate paper with silver chloride or silver iodide then to wash it over with the gallic acid solution just before exposure and again during exposure. Although he came very close to doing so, Reade did not discover the development of a latent image by gallic acid, the credit for which is due to Fox Talbot. Reade did make positive prints of some of his pictures, although he left his "solar mezzotints" of microscopic objects in negative form. Before 1839 he had produced pictures in the camera, including the first recorded photograph of a living person. He fixed his paper negatives and positive prints with "hypo", having read of its action in a chemistry textbook of the day which referred to the work of Sir John Herschel.

Reade never patented any of his findings and only published details of his methods several years later. In April 1839 he exhibited some "solar mezzotints" at the London Institution and later at the Royal Society. Talbot was exhibiting some of his pictures at the Royal Society at the same time, and the two almost surely met and discussed their respective methods, although Talbot later denied this. Reade was often urged to oppose publicly the patents of Talbot but he did not do so until the *Talbot* v. *Laroche* trial in 1854, and then not for his own sake.

Although the materials needed for the calotype process were fairly cheap and the technique quite easy to learn, the process did not become very widely used. Talbot's patents did not help, even amateurs were expected to buy a licence from him before taking calotype pictures. Talbot himself tried very hard to make the process more popular. He sold copies of engravings and "Sun Pictures" of British scenery by way of retail shops throughout the country. In 1843 Fox Talbot set up the first photographic printing establishment in the world, at Reading. There he employed one assistant and later several assistants who produced all the prints for Talbot's publications. They also made up kits of chemicals and prepared paper for amateur use. The first book to be illustrated by actual photographs was *The Pencil of Nature*, produced by Talbot, in four parts from 1844 to 1846. In the introduction to Part I he described how his experiences in Italy in 1833 had caused him to start the experiments which led to the perfection of the calotype.

In spite of its obvious advantage over the daguerreotype process in making large numbers of copies of one photograph possible, the calotype did have two main disadvantages. One was that it required longer exposures in the camera than the daguerreotype did with its later improvements. The other was that the quality of the pictures was inferior, especially in the positive prints, where finer detail became lost when printing through the texture of the paper negatives. Some early photographers preferred the softer effects of the calotypes, however, and some excellent portrait work especially was accomplished by its use.

In 1851 Frederick Scott Archer (1813–57) introduced the wet collodion process, in which silver salts were coated on glass in a film of collodion (nitrocellulose dissolved in an alcohol/ether mixture). The plates were exposed while still wet and produced very clear glass negatives. Fox Talbot held this to be a modification of his process. In 1852 he was persuaded to relinquish part of his patent rights following entreaties by Sir Charles Eastlake, President of the Royal Academy, and Lord Rosse, President of the Royal Society. Still in the belief that his patents covered the collodion process, Talbot retained his rights with regard to professional portrait photography. He issued injunctions against several professional photographers to prevent them from using collodion without a licence from him. Some defied these injunctions and one of them, Sylvester Laroche, tried to prevent Talbot from renewing the patents (the first patent was due to expire in 1855). Talbot therefore filed a lawsuit against Laroche during 1854.

In the *Talbot* v. *Laroche* trial in December 1854 the defence attempted to prove firstly that Talbot should not have patented the calotype anyway, as gallic acid was first used by the Rev. J. B. Reade, and secondly that Talbot's patent did not extend to the use of collodion. Reade gave evidence for the defence. During the trial Talbot denied having met Reade previously, but admitted that he had first heard of the use of gallic acid from the optician Andrew Ross. It was adjudged that because Reade had not published his work first, Talbot was the true inventor of the calotype for the purposes of the patent. A favourable verdict was given to Laroche with regard to the collodion process, however. The use of Archer's process was thenceforward free for general use, as its inventor had intended. Talbot did not renew the calotype patents, and the British patent of the daguerreotype had expired in 1853, so at last all forms of photography could be used in Britain without restrictions by both amateurs and professionals.

During 1852 Fox Talbot perfected and patented a process for making printing blocks directly by photographic means, using a coating of potassium dichromate and gelatine on steel plates. He called this method "Photoglyphic Engraving". The principle of this process is still used today. In his later years Talbot experimented with possible methods of colour photography, but without any success. He died on 17 September 1877 at Lacock Abbey, aged 77.

The most significant year in the early history of photography was undoubtedly 1839. The announcement of Daguerre's success in that January inspired Talbot to publish his results and others to increase their efforts towards perfecting their own independent processes. Thus during March Hippolyte Bayard in France succeeded in producing direct positives in a camera, but only published his methods later. In England Sir John Herschel produced positive and negative pictures, some of them in a camera. He sent a selection of these to the Royal Society, along with his paper describing the use of "hypo". also in March 1839. In September 1839 Herschel took the earliest surviving successful photograph on glass. From 1839 onwards more and more people adopted photography as a hobby or as a means of livelihood. A steady stream of improvements to apparatus and processes has flowed ever since.

SUGGESTIONS FOR FURTHER READING

ELDER, J. M., *The History of Photography*. Trans. Epstein. Columbia University Press, New York, 1945.

GERNSHEIM, H., and GERNSHEIM, G. A., *The History of Photography from the Earliest Use of the Camera Obscura in the 11th Century to 1914*. Oxford University Press, London, 1955.

LECUYER, R., *Histoire de la Photographie*. Baschet, Paris, 1945.

E

CHAPTER 5

SIR CHARLES LYELL, 1797–1875

THERE are two great conflicts between science and religion in the nineteenth century; two great intellectual growing points. The first is the geological conflict, involving the antiquity of the globe and the nature of change in the world. This was essentially Sir Charles Lyell's battle. The second was the biological conflict, in which the protagonist was Charles Darwin. There is a real sense, however, as Darwin himself was only too ready to admit, in which Lyell prepared the way for evolution. He was able to take his stand because he was not only a geologist, pushing forward the frontiers of knowledge in his own chosen field when it was still possible for the single-minded amateur to do so, but he was also a philosopher exploring the relationships of his knowledge with that of other spheres. He, almost alone of the geologists of his time, realized that the accumulation of data was not enough if the philosophical basis of the subject was unsound. His work had the additional dimension needed to make of geology a respectable science and free it once and for all from its mythical moorings. "The front of heaven was not full of fiery shapes at my nativity", he wrote to his fiancée later, when she requested, as fiancées will, autobiographical details. It was, however, at least an event significant for the history of natural science. Who, then, was Charles Lyell, and what combination of opportunities and talents made his life's work possible?

HIS EARLY YEARS

He was a Scot, born on 14 November 1797, the eldest of the ten children of the Laird of Kinnordy in Forfarshire. The opportunities were provided initially by the accident of birth in a cultured and leisured family. His father was a man of wide interests, having worked in a small but useful way in collecting the cryptograms of his native Scotland, and later becoming something of a scholar in the writings of Dante. When the boys were home for the long summer vacations, their father tutored them in the classics in such an enlightened way that Charles often surprised his schoolmasters by his knowledge, not so much of the grammar as of the context and background of the literature. In his father's library he found a collection of books on entomology which launched him on a career of insect collecting at the ripe age of ten; a career which he followed absorbedly as a schoolboy, and later recruited his sisters to collect, document and barter his specimens. It was not unknown, in after years, for visitors to Kinnordy to arrive with hats lined with cork in order to carry off duplicates. More important was his finding of Bakewell's *Geology*, his introduction to the science which was to become his first love and absorbing study. At this first reading, his imagination was already stirred by the idea of the antiquity of the earth.

The talents also were already in evidence in the normal schoolboy who enjoyed the technicalities of a bolster fight and who was often called in to climb after high birds' nests inaccessible to the less agile. First was his power of accurate and thorough observation, already finding an outlet in entomology. All of Lyell's later conclusions and convictions were based on careful and detailed observation of geological facts, and he was irritated by slipshod work. Secondly, he seems to have developed considerable facility in writing and pleasure in composition, for he records that he composed gratuitously in Latin, while at his last school, a mock heroic poem describing a fight between land rats and water rats, using Homer's battle of the frogs and mice as a model. The subject was suggested by the draining of a rat-infested pond in the school grounds, and the poem opened when the water prophet covered with slimy reeds appeared to the King Rat in a dream, "foretelling that the delicious expanse of sweet-scented mud would soon dry-up, and foreboding woes". This literary ease and vigour stood him in good stead when it came to handling what was then essentially a descriptive science, and in no small measure accounts for the success of his work. Lastly, he had a singleness of enthusiasm which enabled him to concentrate his energies and avoid distractions. As a schoolboy he considered that he was inclined to be lazy unless he had some incentive to work.

Another quality, often cited by his detractors, was also evident in the schoolboy and that was his reluctance to enter into a fight. He recalls in his journal the misery that a boy in a boarding school must suffer if he is not prepared to do battle for his rights. At last he was driven to take his stand, and after a bloody battle lasting for five or six hours on two successive days, in which he sustained many injuries, he despatched his adversary to bed. Later, he showed the same reluctance to enter the lists of controversy, so that even his friends were sometimes exasperated by his caution.

The young man of seventeen, then, who went up to Exeter College, Oxford, to read the classics, had been educated in the manner typical of his class, at schools at Ringwood, Salisbury and Midhurst, the latter run on the Winchester pattern. He had spent his vacations in the bosom of his family, then residing at Bartley Lodge in the New Forest, where haymaking lasted through the long summer days, and where each group of trees on the estate was given its own familiar name. He had collected insects with more enthusiasm than scientific system, identifying them by matching them up with the illustrations in *Donovan's Insects*. He had discovered a simple way of descending high trees—always more difficult to climb down than up—by crawling to the flimsy end of a branch until his weight bent it over to within jumping distance of the ground. He knew at sight the eggs of all the local birds. He had rolled stones down the steep moat sides at Old Salop and hunted for chalcedony or quartz when they cracked open at the bottom—his first exercise in field geology—at the age of ten. At Oxford, his taste for geology was to develop with great rapidity.

GEOLOGY IN 1815

In the Oxford of 1815, Buckland, the eccentric first professor of geology, was at the height of his popularity and Lyell was one of the most regular of his students. Buckland was a colourful lecturer, illustrating his reconstructions of the flight of pterodactyls by flapping his clerical coat-tails. He took his students into the field on horseback, and had the gift of enthusing them with his own love of the subject. Lyell never ceased to be grateful to Buckland for his enthusiasm, although he was later to diverge widely from his old professor's views.

The geology that Buckland taught was based on the much venerated system of Abraham Gottlob Werner of Freiburg, which classified rocks according to their mineral content. It viewed earth history, with a fore-shortened time span, as a series of separate creations wiped out in turn by a series of "catastrophes" more violent than anything now experienced by man. After each cataclysm, the world was restocked by the Creator with a new set of living organisms. Noah's flood, as recorded by Moses, was the last of these catastrophes and could be dated at the year 2501 B.C. The present rocks, as we see them, had gradually been laid down from the universal ocean in layers like the coat's of an onion. Thus, the primitive rocks, granite and gneiss were the first to crystallize out from the mother liquor and others were laid down in turn, the most recent being the alluvium and volcanic lava still being deposited. This oversimplified system ignored a number of facts whose cumulative force would be enough to overthrow it. Meanwhile, however, it offered a possible system and science must take as its starting point some hypothesis which can be tested and if necessary proved to be false.

It had already been unsuccessfully attacked by the Scottish philosopher, James Hutton, who published his *Theory of the Earth* in 1795. This involved and obscure work was largely unread, and as is so often the fate of the unread, largely misinterpreted. In it, Hutton claimed that rocks were of two main kinds rather than one; some, the sedimentary rocks, had undoubtedly been laid down in the beds of oceans, but others had been formed by the action of heat and consisted of fused masses which had solidified. He also claimed that there was no geological evidence for catastrophes, and that the natural forces which could be observed in action, when operating over immensely long periods, accounted for the condition of the earth's surface. This at once required a longer time schedule than theologians were prepared to allow. In fact it challenged the whole circumscribed and secure picture of the world as created and directed by God for the benefit of man, and offered instead a bleak and unending abyss of time and change; for Hutton went further and said: "In the economy of the world, I can find no traces of a beginning, no prospect of an end." He was attacked bitterly as a heretic, and his work dismembered and forgotten.

In geological circles then, in 1815, catastrophic doctrines held undisputed sway. All the reputable geologists of Buckland's generation were catastrophists, and it was the policy of the Geological Society, founded in 1807, to eschew controversy as barren and unbecoming, and to collect data which would establish the young science on a firm factual basis. Meanwhile, the most far-reaching development in technique had been incorporated into the study almost unnoticed. This was William Smith's use of fossils to identify and date the different strata. The Wernian method of identification, being purely minera-logical, did not provide a sufficiently fine key to distinguish strata within the broad mineral types, nor did it allow for the fact that the same mineral might be laid down at widely different epochs. William Smith, the "Father of English Geology", was a practical drainage engineer who made use of the fossil record as early as 1795. He published little and never joined the Geological Society, but his maps and specimens were freely available. In 1815 his map of the strata of England and Wales was published, accompanied by a "Memoir to the Map", explaining the method. In it, he distinguished for the first time many of the strata, adopting the familiar local names for the material, such as "cornbrash" and "gault". In the 1820's his method was recognized as the master principle of the science.

Even so, it was a very young science to which Lyell committed himself with such enthusiasm: one in which there was almost everything to learn, in which the method of study, though promising, was still only tentatively applied, and in which the philosophic basis was crude and ready to crumble at the first clearly marshalled attack. By his single-minded industry Lyell was to contribute fact, method and philosophy.

THE DEVELOPMENT OF LYELL'S THOUGHT

For this young man with the enquiring mind, then, geology provided just the frame-work that he needed. From his Oxford days, he looked at scenery skeletally as an anatomist looks at bones. The clarity, insight and independence of his grasp of geological phenomena can be seen in his first interpretation, despatched in a letter to his father from Yarmouth when he was nineteen. He concluded, in a few days of exploration, that the River Yare had changed its course owing to the accumulation of sand in the estuary. He wrote to his father:

> Yarmouth is a delta formed at the mouth of the Yare. When first these sands rose, by the opposition of the sea-tide and river, Norwich was a great seaport (as we find records of), the violence of the tide being kept off by that bank, the estuary filled up with "fluviatile detritus". The Yare then wound through the present marshes, and entered the sea north of Yarmouth (Mr. T. says "No"). The reason that it then turned off at right angles was that, the mouth being stopped by the sea, it was obliged to find a new course, and the north river meeting it there, it flowed with it southward, and entered a little south of the town, then two miles farther off, then four miles at Gorleston, where the pier is which you saw. All these ancient channels I found, and the Doctor confirmed them, though Mr. Turner laughs in spite of facts and tradition.

He went on to examine the spit of sand on which Gorleston stands and discovered the last bed of shingle brought in by the sea 8 feet down in a pit. He concluded that the sand cliff had been built up by wind action and held in place by restharrow and other plants during the last 35 years. Thus his first attempt at interpretation impressed him with the power of the sea to change the coastline decisively in a very short period of time.

This short holiday was the first of many geologizing expeditions. Travel was to be for Lyell, from this time onwards, his chief source of inspiration. Indeed, he regarded it as a necessity if his views were to be sound and broadly based. "We must preach up travelling", he wrote to his colleague Roderick Murchison in January 1829, " . . . as the first, second and third requisites for a modern geologist, in the present adolescent state of the science." As well as Yarmouth, that summer of 1817 found him at Kinnordy and from there he went with two college friends to Staffa and Iona. In the summer of 1818 he had his first opportunity of geologizing on the Continent, then open again to travellers after the Napoleonic wars, and he toured France, Switzerland and Italy with his family. On this tour he frequently went off and roughed it alone for a few days (including one trek of 48 miles, "too much for one day"). In this way he was able to see, among other things, the Glacier de Bossom and the Mere de Glace of Mont Blanc. Avalanches which closed off whole valleys, and torrents capable of washing away bridges and rolling rocks like pebbles again impressed him with the tremendous power of natural forces.

The next decade, from the time he left Oxford to the publication of the *Principles of Geology* in 1830, was to be a period of maturing and of increasing competence and confidence. He was based in London where he was studying and practising law, when his eyesight would allow. Geology was his hobby and delight. He pursued it in the Geological Society which he joined in 1819 and which was to be the forum where his theories would be debated; he pursued it on vacations travelling in Scotland, in Romney Marsh, in the Isle of Wight, in the West Country, and on the Continent in the company variously of Buckland, Constans Prevost and others; he pursued it in Paris in the studios of the great Cuvier and under Deshayes the conchologist; he searched out many of the leading geologists in Italy and Germany. It was all grist to his mill. Geology was more than a hobby: it was a consuming passion. "As to geology having *half* of my heart", he

wrote to his fiancée in 1831, "I hope I shall be able to give my
whole soul to it, with that enthusiasm by which alone any advance
can be made in any science." It is to be hoped that the lady
competing in vain for half a heart found this protestation re-
assuring. He was fast becoming a widely experienced geologist;
and all his experience was pushing him in the same direction,
away from catastrophism and towards his own theory of the
uniformity of natural causes. Crucial in this development were
his friendship with Charles Poulett Scrope, and his tour of the
Auvergne, Italy and Sicily to study river valleys, volcanoes and
tertiary deposits.

C. P. Scrope joined the Geological Society in 1824, and in
1825 he became joint secretary with Lyell. The two had much
in common, and the ensuing friendship was stimulating, fruitful
and life-long, although Scrope after his marriage diverted his
energies to public work. Scrope had already made a detailed
comparative study of several volcanic areas on the Continent.
From his examination of the Auvergne, a region of extinct
volcanoes, he reached the controversial conclusion that river
valleys were caused not simultaneously when the waters of the
Deluge receded, as catastrophic doctrine taught, but by slow
continuous denudation over long periods. This came close, once
again, to Hutton's views on the uniformity of natural causes.
Scrope completed his account in April 1822 under the title
Memoir on the Geology of Central France. This factual account was
unfortunately not published until 1827, for Scrope hastened back
to Italy to view again an area of living volcanoes, and witnessed
the "stupendous eruption" of Vesuvius in October 1822. As a
result, he published first his much more speculative *Considerations
on Volcanoes* in 1825. It was received in geological circles with
incredulity, as a series of wild speculations unfounded upon fact.
Lyell, reviewing the *Memoir* which followed in 1827, suggested
that if this valuable document had been published first, Scrope's
speculations would have received a fairer hearing.

But Lyell, already in 1827 at work on his own *magnum opus*, was
much excited by Scrope's work and the discussion they had

together, especially as his own thinking had been moving independently in the same direction for some years. His first paper, read before the Geological Society in 1825, "On a recent Formation of Freshwater Limestone in Forfarshire, and on some recent Deposits of Freshwater Marl" had been a refutation of Cuvier's classic doctrine. Cuvier held that the limestone of the ante-diluvian world was of a totally different kind from that laid down subsequently from fresh water. The former was crystalline, without shells, and having plant remains embedded in it. He concluded that the fresh water of the ancient world possessed properties not observed in the water of modern lakes. Lyell, on his visits to Kinnordy from 1817, had been able to examine the deposits of small lakes which were being drained and quarried for marling the land. He found that the calcareous deposits beneath recently formed peat passed imperceptibly into a solid crystalline rock, containing the stems and fruits of the freshwater plant *Chara*; in short that from a modern freshwater lake, containing only a small proportion of calcium salts, a limestone with all the characteristics of Cuvier's ancient type had been deposited. He had already, as we have seen, been impressed by the power of natural forces. Now, Scrope was suggesting that river valleys were formed by slow continuous action over long periods; action deemed totally inadequate by Buckland and the catastrophists. In his review of Scrope's *Memoir*, Lyell pointed out that it should be possible to settle the question empirically from the conditions in the Auvergne. He determined to go and see for himself.

Accordingly, abandoning for the moment his writing, he set off in May 1828 for Clermont Ferrand, accompanied by Roderick Murchison and his wife, on what was to be the most formative tour of his career. He was to return to London in February 1829 having served his apprenticeship—a master of his craft.

It is impossible to read the journals and letters of this time without being aware of mounting excitement, of purposeful and economic activity emerging from somewhat fumbling beginnings, and of gradually crystalizing judgements and convictions. Even the weather was favourable, from the sunny rainless days of the

Auvergne, to the day in December when he climbed Etna—the last man of the season to do so, for the following day the routes were closed by snow. But let him speak for himself. To his mother, in a letter dated 11 June, he wrote from Mont Dore:

> We have been so actively employed, I may really say so laboriously, that I assure you I can with great difficulty find a moment to write a letter. This morning we got off, after breakfast at 5 o'clock, on horseback, to return from St. Amand to this; arrived at seven o'clock. But one day we rode fifty-five miles, which I shall take care shall be the last experiment of that kind, as even the old Leics. fox-hunter was nearly done up with it. But I have really gained strength so much that I believe that I and my eyes were never in such condition before; and I am sure that six hours in bed, which is all we allow, and exercise all day long for the body, and geology for the mind, with plenty of the *vin du pays*, which is good here, is the best thing that can be invented in this world, for my health and happiness . . . Indeed I really think I am most profitably employed on this tour, and as long as things go on as well as they do now, I should be very sorry to leave off; particularly as, from our plan of operation, which is that of comparison of the structure of different parts of the country, we work on with a continually increasing power, and in the last week have with the same exertion done at least twice as much in the way of discovery, and in enlarging our knowledge of what others had done, as in any preceding.

In two months they had collected more original data, Lyell thought, than had then been published on any part of France so far from Paris. They continued south, and when at Nice, Murchison had to rest from a "severe attack" (of malaria?) they took the opportunity to write up a paper on the excavation of valleys— a paper intended to "reform the Geological Society, and afterward the world, on this hitherto-not-in-the-least-degree-understood subject".

From Nice he wrote to his father, reporting progress and future plans:

> The whole tour has been rich, as I had anticipated (and in a manner which M. had not) in those analogies between existing Nature and the effects of causes in remote areas which it will be the great object of my work to point out. I scarcely despair now, so much do these evidences of modern action increase upon us as we go south (towards the more recent volcanic seat of action), of *proving* the positive identity of the causes now operating with those of former times . . . But I feel, as Murchison says, that if I wish to get out, by November year, such a book as will decidedly do me credit, and probably be a source of profit, it is to the south of the Po

I should hasten, and before Christmas everything might be done. He said yesterday "At Milan or Verona, in three or four weeks or thereabouts, the operations connected with our paper will be over, but Sicily is for your views the great end: there are the most modern analogies, volcanic, marine, elevatory, subsiding, etc. I know the island as a soldier, and if you make straight for Etna, will just time it right for work, for the season will be exactly suitable". I feel so decidedly that three months' more steady work will carry me through all, and tell greatly both to the despatch of finishing my work, as well as to the power I shall have in writing it, that I should greatly repent if I did not do all in my power to accomplish it now.

And so it fell out. He parted from the Murchisons in Padua, and made for the tertiary deposits of the Sub-Apennines, and the volcanoes of Sicily. By that time he knew exactly what to look for and who best could help him. From Professor Guidotti in Parma, he learnt much of the fossil shells of Italy, and came away with a collection of Sub-Apennine fossils identical with species now living in the Mediterranean. He continued to Rome and Naples; then to Ischra, where he found modern marine shells at a great height on the mountain side, thus proving an elevation of 2600 ft, "since the Med. was peopled with the very species of shell-fish which have now the honour of living with, or being eaten by us". He went on to Sicily and Etna where he sketched the Valle del Boue, while his boots were roasting in hot ashes and his hands freezing in the December gale. He returned via Palermo, Naples, Geneva, and lastly Paris, where he sought the collaboration of Deshayes, the conchologist, in identifying his Sicilian shells. He was in London again in February 1829.

The tour had more than fulfilled his expectations. Very early in his progress through the Auvergne, he had become convinced of the soundness of Scrope's views on river valleys. One irrefutable test case he had found exactly as he had hoped, which settled the question to his satisfaction. Not far from Clermont Ferrand, and unknown to both Scrope and Buckland, a stream of basaltic lava had flowed down the valley of the Sioule, choking it and causing a lake to be formed. The valley had been originally a defile of gneiss, and the river gradually cut through at the junction of basalt and gneiss, wearing away the softer gneiss to a depth of 150 ft and 85 ft into the underlying granite. The basalt was left as a towering cliff on one bank, and a bed of pebbles between the basalt and the gneiss marked the level of the ancient river bed. He was certain that no deluge had formed that valley.

But the settling of this controversy assumed the importance of a mere incident in the perspective of the whole tour. Italy and Sicily provided him with evidence of the gradual elevation of considerable mountains since modern fauna had inhabited the Mediterranean. He began to work out his scheme for dating all the then-known tertiary formations according to the proportion of living to extinct species of mollusc that they contained. He was convinced that the modern analogies that he could observe there were adequate to account for geological phenomena. From Naples he wrote to Murchison:

> My work is in part written, and all planned. It will not pretend to give even an abstract of all that is known in geology, but it will endeavour to establish the *principle of reasoning* in the science; and all my geology will come in as illustration of my views of those principles . . . neither more nor less than that *no causes whatever* have from the earliest time to which we can look back, to the present, ever acted but those *now acting*; and that they never acted with different *degrees of energy from that which they now exert*.

It was to the defence of these principles of uniformity and the overthrow of catastrophism that he was now committed. Indeed the battle was already joined when he returned to London, for Murchison had fired the opening shot in his absence, and read their joint paper on the excavation of valleys in the Auvergne before the Geological Society. The "Old Guard" had recognized it as a declaration of war.

In attempting to overthrow catastrophic doctrines, Lyell was fully aware that he had set himself no small task. Indeed, had his love of geology been less single-minded, he might well have shrunk from such a task, since it forced him to work against the grain of his own character in a number of ways. He was reluctant to stand to a fight, even as a schoolboy; he was cautious in committing himself to a definite position, short of proof positive— a trait which his legal training had done nothing to diminish; and his natural courtesy would not willingly give offence either to the "prejudices of the age" or more especially to men who were his personal friends and teachers, and for whose work in some areas he had considerable respect. But he was convinced that the Deluge presented an insuperable obstacle in the way of progress. He returned to London in the mood of a man attempting nothing less than the emancipation of his first love from intolerable tyranny. He was determined to free geology from the parental control of natural theology, as in turn each newly differentiated science has to be freed. This is the mood of a man who does not contemplate failure. In fact, it is hard to resist the conclusion that, for a man of pacific nature, he derived a good deal of enjoyment and exhilaration from the passages of arms in the Geological Society.

The immediate problems of 1829 were those of presentation and tactics, and they were carefully planned. He had before him the object lesson of Hutton's earlier failure with ignominy to gain a hearing for similar controversial views, and he was anxious to avoid a similar fate. Accordingly, he concentrated on readableness and clarity of style. "I must write what will be read", he had written to a friend, as early as 1826. And he determined to underplay the more unacceptable corollaries of his findings. "I assure you I have been so cautious", he wrote to his sister, "that two friends tell me I shall *only* offend the ultras." He worked fast. The first volume of the *Principles of Geology* was in the hands of the printer by December 1829; Volume II followed two years later in January 1832; and Volume III in May 1833. What, then, did the *Principles* say, and how far was he successful in presenting his case?

VOLUME I AND THE UNIFORMITARIAN DEBATE

The first volume of the *Principles* was a treatise on the nature of change in the inorganic world. It was written in its final form in a matter of months, under great pressure and excitement, and it launched his theory of the uniformity of natural causes throughout geological time. It was this volume, therefore, which made the main impact, and which contained his most decisive and controversial thought.

He staked out his position on the title page: "Principles of Geology, being an attempt to explain the former Changes of the Earth's Surface, by reference to causes now in Operation." He had to convince a geological world committed to a foreshortened time-span, and to a world history cataclysmic in its progressions, that nature had *not* in times past been "parsimonious of time and prodigal of violence". He had to convince men's imaginations as well as their intellects that slow and gradual, and often insignificant agents, given vast stretches of time, could bring about the vast changes that the earth had clearly undergone. The last two-thirds of the book, therefore, deal with a factual account of these "causes now in operation". This was an aspect of geology which had been almost totally neglected, and by virtue of which the book was greeted with enthusiasm as laying the foundation of a new branch of the study. "Whewell of Cambridge", he wrote with satisfaction to his sister Marianne in November 1830, "has done me no small service by giving out at his University that I have discovered a new set of powers in Nature which might be termed 'Geological Dynamics'. He is head tutor at Trinity, and has more influence than any individual, unless it be Sedgwick."

In this part, he divided the causes of change in the inorganic world into aqueous and igneous. In the chapters on aqueous agents, he began with the power of running water in springs and rivers; power for destruction, as in the gouging out of valleys, and power for transport and deposition, as in the formation of deltas and lake deposits. He went on to deal with ocean currents and tides, both for erosion and for deposition. As igneous agents, he treated of volcanoes and earthquakes. All were given the same meticulous treatment—often with the vivid details of an eye-witness. All his geological experience was utilized, from the observations of the undergraduate of 19 on the dunes of the Norfolk coast, to those of the lawyer of 31 on the summit of Etna. All was authentically presented, and supplemented by his thorough knowledge of the literature of the subject. It made exciting and fascinating reading.

The earlier chapters of the work contain the more controversial material. He had long been of the opinion that the "diluvian humbug", as he was pleased to call it privately, could best be attacked indirectly through an historical sketch. Accordingly, in the introductory chapters, he outlined the history of the subject from its Egyptian and Greek origins, down to the controversy between Werner's and Hutton's views. "If I have said more than some will like, yet I give you my word that full *half* of my history and comments was cut out, and even many facts; because either I, or Stokes, or Broderip, felt that it was anticipating twenty or thirty years of the march of honest feeling to declare it undisguisedly." And, in fact, ironically enough, the only person who objected to his historical sketch was Dr. Fitton of Edinburgh, who took him to task for not having given Hutton sufficient credit for his priority.

In Chapter 5, "Review of the causes which have retarded the progress of Geology", he began to grasp the nettle directly and this is one of his most eloquent passages, in the rather heroic Victorian manner, full of analogy and allusion. The first difficulty, he claimed, was the mistaken idea of the short duration of past time. This inevitably had the effect of telescoping events and exaggerating violence, just as would happen if the whole history of a nation should be mistakenly thought to have been condensed into a period of 100 years. But modern studies of organic remains in the rocks had forced geologists to intercalate vast stretches of time into the history of the globe. Secondly, he continued, our position as observers on the dry land of only one-quarter of the globe, gave us a partial and biassed view of the whole. Some intelligent amphibious creature who could examine ocean beds, or some gnome delving in the rocks, would have a totally different, and in some ways more accurate account to give. Thirdly, the ancient idea of the universality of the ocean had been exploded by finding fossils of land plants corresponding in time with all the successive races of marine creatures. Hence modern research (in

1829) had removed entirely some obstacles to a view of the uniformity of secondary causes.

There were, however, two obstacles remaining which he was to find a constant source of embarrassment, since the case for the uniformity of causes implied a fundamental changelessness. It could allow long cycles of change. It could not allow great trends of change by which new conditions came permanently into being. Still less could it allow progress. Yet on the inorganic side there was the commonly accepted theory that the globe was gradually cooling. He himself could not doubt the evidence that the Northern Hemisphere had been much hotter in times past, when tree ferns had flourished far to the north. On the organic side there was the apparently increasing complexity of living things as revealed by the fossil record. Both of these progressions he denied in the following chapters.

The inorganic progression he dealt with, entirely to his own satisfaction and within his own terms, by his theory of the effect of the relative positions of land and sea on climate. The effect of large land masses near the poles, he argued, would be to cool down the whole globe. In former times large equatorial land masses, acting as radiators, had raised the temperature. If these conditions should return, he continued, "then might those genera of animals return, of which the memorials are preserved in the ancient rocks of our continents. The huge iguanodon might reappear in the woods, and the ichthyosaur in the sea, while the pterodactyle might flit again through umbrageous groves of tree-ferns."

The organic progression was more troublesome, and his handling of it the least satisfactory part of his work—inevitably so for he was essentially in a false position. "Progressionists" in nineteenth-century parlance, claimed that each creation had been more advanced than the previous one. The globe was first inhabited by cryptogams, accompanied by zoophytes and molluscs. Then came the age of ferns and reptiles, and this was followed by flowering plants with birds, mammals, and finally man. This sequence, accepted by hindsight as substantially correct, had no evolutionary connotations. No development from one set of organisms to the next was envisaged, and the theory was merely a variant of catastrophism. As such, Lyell attacked it with all his skill. It was just possible in 1830, owing to the incompleteness of the fossil record, and the inaccuracy of some identifications, to deny that the evidence indicated a progression of this kind. This Lyell did, making an exception only in the case of man, whom he believed to be so recent as never to have seen a living mammoth. He maintained this increasingly uncomfortable position for over thirty years. It was to place him, later, in much the same position *vis-à-vis* Darwin and the next generation, as the older generation now found itself *vis-à-vis* Lyell himself. The dilemma was not to be resolved until Darwin provided a *mechanism* for change in the organic world, so that the evolutionary progression could be assimilated to the province of natural causes. Lyell, in 1829, could take only a negative view. He found evidence for the extinction of species. On their mode of origin he had nothing positive to say.

The first volume of the *Principles* was an immediate success. It was hailed as a masterpiece by enthusiasts and opponents alike, and lionized from the start. The 1500 copies of the first edition were quickly sold out, and a second edition was published in 1832, together with Volume II. Lyell knew nothing of its success for several months, for true to his determination to avoid time-wasting controversy, he had set off for the Pyrenees as soon as he had corrected the proofs. The reaction of the literary world may be summarized by the remark of Captain Basil Hall, traveller and author, who greeted him on his return to London with the words "Lyell, I never thought you had it in you to write such a book. I don't mean as a geologist, but as a writer". Adam Sedgwick (known to his Cambridge students as the "First of Men") spoke for the scientific world in his Presidential Address to the Geological Society, in February 1831, when he said "Were I to tell him of the instruction I received from every chapter of his work, and of the delight with which I rose from the perusal of the whole, I might seem to flatter rather than to speak the language of sober criticism."

Lyell's nervousness about the reactions of the theological world proved largely unnecessary, owing to his cautious handling of the controversial issues. By great good fortune, the *Principles* appeared under the aegis of that organ of orthodoxy, *The Quarterly Review*, for which the sympathetic and discerning Scrope had been invited to write the review. In fact a certain amount of collusion took place between author and reviewer as to tactics. Lyell managed, therefore, to avoid the *odium theologicum* which had been the downfall of Hutton; so much so, indeed, that in March 1831 he was invited by a panel including three bishops to accept the chair of Geology in the newly founded Anglican King's College, London. Scrope was to comment, "If the news be true, and your opinions are to be taken at once into the bosom of the Church, instead of contending against that party for half a century, then, indeed, shall we make a step at once of fifty years in the science—in such a miracle will I believe when I see it performed."

But this general approbation did not prevent the catastrophists from rallying at once to a counter-attack. Scrope, who was no catastrophist, had already voiced a doubt about the fitness of denying progression in the inorganic world. He also distinguished between the efficiency of causes now in operation to bring about change, and the further conclusion that such changes had never "from all eternity" varied in intensity or proportion. Other critical reviews came from Sedgwick and Whewell. Sedgwick made the same criticism as Scrope in his Presidential Address, adding that it was presumptuous to assume that nature's operations were confined to our knowledge of them. This was, of course, unanswerable, and Lyell himself, in a different context, had been at pains to point out how partial was our view of geological phenomena. Sedgwick, however, recanted handsomely and publicly on the specific issue of the Mosaic Deluge. This, of course, made his remaining criticisms all the more forceful, and Lyell recognized him as the most trenchant of his critics.

Whewell's review, in *The British Critic*, Lyell also recognized as both pertinent and influential, although Whewell was an historian of science rather than a practical scientist. So firmly entrenched was catastrophism that Whewell could write in 1832, ". . . . we conceive that Mr. Lyell will find it a harder task than he appears to contemplate to overturn this established belief". In reviewing Volume I in 1831, he adopted a tone of gentle ridicule, so confident was he of the outcome. But his criticism was to the point. Lyell, he said, was committed to defend three theses; that known causes give an adequate account, firstly of the mechanical effects which the geologist must explain, secondly of climatic changes in the history of the globe, and thirdly of changes from one set of organisms to another. On the first point, he said, Lyell had produced a valuable thesis; on the second an ingenious theory; on the third nothing at all. It was a very fair summary. But, despite his confidence, Whewell's tone when he reviewed the second volume in 1832 was much moderated. Ridicule was abandoned, and the whole question of the efficiency of secondary causes was left open.

The most reluctant to moderate was, of course, Buckland, whose first reaction to the heresies of his pupil was simple wrath. But the weight of detailed fact was against him, and he had to resort to expediencies more and more wild to preserve the appearances. At one stage, he had recourse to no less than three universal floods. Lyell and Murchison watched his antics with no little interest and amusement. They watched especially for the publication of his "Bridgewater Treatise", which was to reconcile Genesis and Geology, and which was an unconscionable time a-writing, and caused its author much heart-searching. It appeared finally in 1836—the "Bridge-over-the-Water" as Murchison irreverently called it, and Lyell added that he could not trust himself upon it, though it was better constructed than he expected. It sold out, however, in spite of them—5000 copies in all.

But by 1840, the Flood as a universal geological agent was no longer respectable among scientists. Of the older generation, Sedgwick was converted, Whewell had moderated his tone, and Buckland had attempted to bluff his way out. There would certainly be die-hards for the rest of the century, but for men of science the controversy was virtually dead. There would be no succeeding generation committed to a literal interpretation of the Mosaic account of geology. Lyell's work would be for the rising generation—for Joseph Hooker, Charles Darwin, Thomas Huxley—its starting point and its accepted vocabulary. Lyell had done what he set out to do. The philosophic issues had received definition. Some remained for settlement, but the realm of discourse would henceforth be rational. The publication of Volume I of the *Principles* marked the occupation of a terrain which had been probed by Hutton in 1795. The process had taken half a century. It shows how vital to the progress of science is a climate of opinion in which growth is possible.

VOLUME II AND THE THEORY OF EVOLUTION

If the first volume of the *Principles* marked the consolidation of a position, the second volume offered a new probe into the nature of change in the organic world; a probe as partial and inconclusive, and in some ways inconsistent, as Hutton's had been. Yet it was to pave the way for the theory of evolution, and to prove seminal in the thinking of Darwin himself.

Lyell's look at the organic world was as dynamic and fresh as his look at the inorganic had been, and opened up the discussion of the phenomena of life in an entirely new way. "No-one", wrote Whewell, "twenty years ago would have conceived it possible that a work on 'The Principles of Geology' should appear, replete with discussions such as those into which Professor Lyell here enters."

He discussed in detail first of all Lamarck's theory of "transformism" and discarded it largely on the grounds of the fixity of species; this, not because he was unaware of variation, but because he thought that there were limits to the amount of variation possible in any species. He then ranged widely over the whole field of the geographical distribution of plants and animals. He discussed with detailed ingenuity their methods of transport by wind and water. He considered the conditions under which a species might prosper or become extinct, and the whole balance of nature. He pointed out that different areas of the globe supported distinct groups of plants and animals, representing supposed foci of creation, or zoological provinces. He discussed the whole economy of nature, showing how changing conditions might favour one species to the detriment of others, and how the introduction of new species into an area might upset the balance. He showed how the organic world in its turn modified the underlying strata, and discussed the formation of fossils.

Even more germane to Darwin's later work was his awareness of the competitive struggle for survival, an idea which he accredited to Augustin Pyramus de Candolle in the following significant quotation: "All the plants of a given country", says De Candolle, in his usual spirited style, "are at war one with another. The first which establish themselves by chance in a particular spot, tend, by the mere occupancy of space, to exclude other species—the greater choke the smaller, the longest livers replace those which last for a shorter period, the more prolific gradually make themselves masters of the ground, which species multiplying more slowly would otherwise kill."

"Nothing", wrote Whewell, "can be more striking than the picture given by our author of the mutual wars of the different tribes of plants and animals, their struggles for food, their powers of diffusion, their relation to man, and the wide and sweeping changes which these phenomena have produced and are producing in the face of animated nature."

In fact, in 1832, by marshalling all the facts concerning variation and distribution of species, Lyell came within an ace of stumbling on the idea of natural selection himself. He clearly understood that changing conditions had caused species to become extinct. He could not satisfy himself as to the origin of new species, though he admitted, when pressed by Sedgwick, that he believed they were continually being created, even if in the nature of the case the evidence for it was practically impossible to find. Two considerations prevented him then, and for many years to come, from placing an evolutionary interpretation on his facts: the first was his view that the fossil record revealed variety but not progression, and the second was his belief in the fixity of species.

This then, Volume II of the *Principles*, was the treatise that awaited Charles Darwin at Monte Video when he rejoined *H.M.S. Beagle* there in November 1832, after his journey into the interior of South America. That Darwin, like Whewell, was much struck by De Candolle's idea of the "war of nature", there can be no doubt, for he refers to it in the first famous pencil sketch of his theory in 1842. Meanwhile, for him, doubts were raised as to the fixity of species when he noted the variations in species of insect caused by isolation in the Galapagos Islands. In 1836 he returned to England and made the acquaintance of Lyell.

Darwin was fully sensible of his debt to Lyell. It was a debt of method, of matter, and later of personal advice and affection. The young man of 22—eleven years Lyell's junior—who set out on board the *Beagle* after an undistinguished career at Cambridge was a very callow scientist indeed. The voyage was to be as formative as was Lyell's earlier journey to the Auvergne. In the quarters of the little ten-gun brig, Darwin studied and thoroughly adopted Lyell's first volume. He recalls his introduction to the book in his autobiography.

"When (I was) starting on the voyage of the *Beagle*, the sagacious Henslow, who, like all other geologists, believed at that time in successive cataclysms, advised me to get and study the first volume of the *Principles*, which had then just been published, but on no account to accept the views therein advocated. How differently would anyone now speak of the *Principles*! I am proud to remember that the first place, namely St. Jago in the Cape de Verde Archipelago, in which I geologized convinced me of the infinite superiority of Lyell's views over those advocated in any other work known to me".

It became his "own true love", and he confessed that the reading of the book entirely altered the quality of his mind. "I always feel as if my books came half out of Lyell's brain", he wrote later.

On his return to England, he sought out Lyell with the enthusiasm of a disciple, and at once became his staunchest supporter in geological circles. The ensuing friendship was life-long, and Lyell had an important part to play in the launching of *The Origin of Species*.

Darwin began collecting data concerning variation as soon as he returned to England. He looked to Lyell for his working model. "After my return to England", he wrote, "it appeared to me that by following the example of Lyell in Geology, and by collecting all facts which bore in any way on the variation of animals and plants under domestication and native, some light might perhaps be thrown on the whole subject. My first notebook was opened in July 1837." But apart from the pencil sketch of 1842, amplified in 1844, Darwin took no further action until urged by Lyell and other close friends, who feared he would be anticipated. This was in 1856, and Darwin began work on a massive treatise. He was barely half-way through when disaster overtook him, in the shape of Wallace's paper on natural selection arriving for his consideration. In dismay, he turned to Lyell for advice. "I never saw a more striking coincidence; if Wallace had my MS. sketch written out in 1842 he could not have made a better short abstract! Even his terms now stand as heads of my chapters", he wrote. Lyell, in this emergency, is seen at his very best—just, tactful, effective, honourable and concerned. He was able to convince Darwin that his name should be coupled with Wallace's in the presentation of the theory—a solution in which Wallace fully agreed. So it came about that the theory of natural selection was presented to the Linnaean Society by Lyell and Hooker on 1 July 1858; Wallace's brief paper, and extracts from Darwin's treatise of 1844, in the absence of both authors. Urged by Lyell and Hooker, Darwin then settled down to write *The Origin of Species* based on the earlier versions of 1844 and 1856. "It cost me thirteen months and ten days' hard labour", he wrote. It was published in November 1859.

The original meeting of the Linnaean Society had caused surprisingly little stir. The publication of *The Origin of Species* aroused the passions of the scientific and theological world. Lyell was at the famous Oxford meeting of the British Association, and he gave the following lively account of that historic fracas in a letter to Sir Charles Bunbury, his brother-in-law:

> I was not able to attend the section of Zoology and Botany (Henslow in the Chair) when first Owen and Huxley, and on a later day the Bishop of Oxford and Huxley, had a spar, and on the latter occasion young Lubbock and Joseph Hooker declared their adhesion to Darwin's theory . . .
>
> The Bishop of Oxford asked whether Huxley was related by his grandfather's or grandmother's side to an Ape. Huxley replied (I heard several varying versions of this shindy) that if he had his choice of an ancestor, whether it should be an ape, or one who having received a scholastic education should use his logic to mislead an untutored public, and should treat not with argument but with ridicule the facts and reasoning adduced in support of a grave and serious philosophical question, he would not hesitate for a moment to choose the ape! Many blamed Huxley for his irreverent freedom; but still more of those I heard talk of it, and among them Falconer, assures me the Vice-Chancellor Jeune (a liberal) declared that the Bishop got no more than he deserved.

If Lyell encouraged Darwin, however, and followed his career with sympathy and interest, Darwin watched hopefully for his "old master's" conversion to his views. It was not forthcoming for seven years after the publication of *The Origin*. In the interval Lyell was preoccupied with his last great work on a closely related subject—*The Antiquity of Man*, published in 1863. This also required revision of his earlier views on the recency of man.

His reluctance to "go the whole orang", as he himself wryly put it, is understandable, for as late as 1851, in his Presidential Address to the Geological Society, he was arguing against "progressionism", with all its catastrophic associations. In fact, the idea of evolution presented a breach in the philosophic position for which he had fought so hard as a young man. In March 1863 he wrote to Darwin, "In the new 'Year Book of Facts' for 1863, of Timbs, you will see my portrait, and a sketch of my career, and how I am the champion of anti-transmution."

That this was for Lyell a genuine *crise de foie* and not mere prevarication as has sometimes been suggested, is clear from his correspondence. Part of his difficulty was his belief in the fixity of species. He was wholly averse from the idea that offspring could be referrable to distinct species from the parent. And how was it possible, he pertinently asked Joseph Hooker back in 1856, to account for the distribution of some species—like *Lysimachia vulgaris*, which had turned up in the Australian Alps—in scattered pockets over the globe? It was altogether contrary to the laws of chance that their evolution should follow the same course in widely separated areas.

His long resistance to the idea of progression in the fossil record was more perverse, and he was guilty of some distortion of the evidence here; especially as by an intellectual sleight of hand he was using precisely a progression to date the tertiary strata. He seized with alacrity on any fossil evidence which could be used against progressionism—supposed mole-type creatures found in the upper colite, and grasses in the coal—although he was forced to admit that the absence of mammalia in the coal was a strong point for the progressive view.

But the facts were gradually accumulating against him, and inch by inch he moved reluctantly into Darwin's camp. When *The Antiquity of Man* came out in 1863, he wrote to Hooker, "(Darwin) seems much disappointed that I do not go farther with him, or do not speak out more. I can only say that I have spoken out to the full extent of my present convictions, and even beyond my state of *feeling*, as to man's unbroken descent from the brutes." But still it was a choice, as one of Darwin's reviewers put it, between "modified mud or modified monkey"—"a great come-down from the 'archangel ruined' ", wrote Lyell. In 1864 he gave the after-dinner speech at the Royal Society Anniversary, commemorating the award of the Copley Medal to Darwin. "It was somewhat of a confession of faith as to the 'Origin' ", he reported to Darwin. "I said I had been forced to give up my old faith without thoroughly seeing my way to a new one." In the end, he went the whole orang in the tenth edition of *The Principles* published in 1868, when he was 69.

But he never went so far as to "deify natural selection", as he accused Huxley and Darwin of doing. To him it was always a subordinate secondary cause, working on variations produced by the Creative Mind, "to which all the wonders of the organic world must be referred". "I think the old 'creation' is almost as much required as ever, but of course, it takes a new form if Lamarck's views improved by yours are adopted", he had written to Darwin in 1863.

This was almost certainly his final position. For him at least the old creation was as much required as ever. Sir Charles Lyell, at the age of 70, still looked out on the natural world that he had loved and explored all his life with the simplicity of a child, and found it a place of wonder. This intellectual journey, occupying all of forty years, was no mean counterpart for the physical journey of one who had "preached up travelling" in his youth, and been a great traveller all his life.

VOLUME III AND LYELL'S GEOLOGICAL WORK

Lyell regarded the first two volumes of the *Principles* as preliminary treatises necessary to clear the ground before dealing with pure geology. Until he had established the nature of change in the inorganic and organic worlds, it was hardly possible to assess the validity of geological evidence. Hence Volume III is the least controversial, and in some ways the most durable, since, once his case was established, the first two were no longer necessary in their polemical form.

Volume III is an analysis of the arrangement of the materials composing the earth's crust; primary, secondary, and tertiary rocks. He first established the method of dating the strata by a small-scale analogy, easily verified. In the bed of a lake layers are to be found, perhaps peat, overlying shell marl, with layers of marl and clay below. The layers lie in order of deposition, with the oldest at the bottom and the most recent at the top. At any point in the lake, the layers would be in the same order, varying perhaps in thickness, with even an occasional omission, but substantially the same. Scaling up his model, he explained that similar deposition had occurred in the beds of oceans, to form the secondary stratified rocks—limestones, clays, and chalk, etc.— of the present continents. In addition to these rocks, he distinguished volcanic rocks of igneous origin, and more ancient or primary rocks, such as granite, of a crystalline, usually unstratified nature, containing no organic remains and often forming the core of great mountain ranges. Finally, he described more recent tertiary rocks of more friable nature, containing marine and often freshwater and terrestrial fossils as well. These deposits occupied limited areas, in positions similar to lakes, gulfs and estuaries, and in all cases were found overlying the chalk. The problem that such deposits presented being discontinuous, was one of chronology. How could their relative ages be determined?

The first tertiary deposit to be examined was that of the Paris Basin, described by Cuvier and Brongniart in 1811 (*Environs de Paris*). Here marine and freshwater deposits alternated, and some strata contained extinct land-living mammals. Next, the tertiary deposits of the London Basin and Hampshire were examined, and found to contain a great variety of fossils of the same species as those of the Paris Basin, although the mineral bases were very different in the two countries: blue clay in Paris, and white limestone in England. Meanwhile, in Italy, it had long been realized that the Sub-Apennines, flanking the Apennines throughout the peninsular, overlay the secondary rocks. Now these tertiary deposits were examined, and it was determined that almost half of the fossil remains represented species still living in the Mediterranean, unlike those of the Paris Basin which were largely extinct.

The next step was the discovery in the basin of the Loire of formations which could be determined as more recent than the Paris deposits. This was possible because the uppermost Parisian stratum formed an unbroken platform between the two river valleys, and was the lowest of the series in the Loire.

These same French deposits could further be dated as older than the Sub-Apennines, since the fossil remains they contained were the same as those of the strata on which the Sub-Apennines lay. Thus a series of three could be made out.

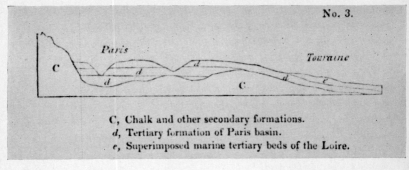

C, Chalk and other secondary formations.
d, Tertiary formation of Paris basin.
e, Superimposed marine tertiary beds of the Loire.

PLATE 13. Strata of the Paris Basin as seen in a section of the Loire Valley.

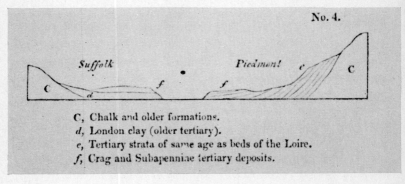

C, Chalk and older formations.
d, London clay (older tertiary).
e, Tertiary strata of same age as beds of the Loire.
f, Crag and Subapennine tertiary deposits.

PLATE 14. Strata of the Paris Basin as seen in a section from Suffolk
to Piedmont. (From the *Principles of Geology*)

He digressed here, to summarize the types of evidence that a
geologist may use to determine chronology. The first and simplest
is superposition, but it is not always available. In addition, the
mineral content of the rock and the organic remains may be used.
Of these two, organic remains are more reliable. Living creatures
are more widely distributed than minerals at any given time.
As illustration of this, he cited the Mediterranean, which supports
throughout the same fauna, although its great rivers, the Nile, the
Rhone and the Po, bring down deposits of different minerals.

But even living things cannot be entirely relied upon, since at the boundaries of zoological provinces two distinct fauna would be met with. The Red Sea, for instance, at the present time supports a fauna entirely different from that of the Mediterranean, though separated from it only by the Suez isthmus.

THE GEOLOGICAL PERIODS

Era	Period	Named by
Quaternary	Recent Pleistocene	Charles Lyell, 1839
Tertiary	Pliocene Miocene Oligocene Eocene	Charles Lyell, 1833 Charles Lyell, 1833 Heinrich von Beyrich, 1854 Charles Lyell, 1833
Secondary	Cretaceous Jurassic Triassic	Omalius d'Halloy, 1822 Christian Leopold von Buch, 1839 Friedrich August von Alberti, 1834
Primary	Permain Carboniferous Devonian Silurian Ordovician Cambrian	Roderick Murchison, 1841 Richard Kirwan, 1799 R. Murchison and Adam Sedgwick, 1837 R. Murchison, 1835 Charles Lapworth, 1879 Adam Sedgwick, 1836

He then returned to the tertiary formations, and launched his own classification. It was based on the proportion of fossils in the rocks which could be identified as living species. He used only molluscs, as being the most reliable fossils. They are widely distributed, fossilized in large numbers without damage, and geologically speaking they are species of long duration. Moreover, some species are confined to salt water, others to fresh water, and yet others to land. The whole classification depended on the accuracy and consistency of the identifications, and for this he had turned to Deshayes, who had made the original identifications of the French deposits. He distinguished four periods in the time between the laying down of the chalk and the appearance of man. These were the newer and older Pliocene, the Miocene, and the Eocene periods. He took great care in the coining of these terms, and consulted Whewell on their exact form. His care was fully justified, for they are now part of the international language of science.

The most recent deposits were the Pliocene. "We derive the term Pliocene from πλειων major, and καινος recens, as the major part of the fossil testacea of this epoch are referable to recent species", he explained. The newer Pliocene deposits were those of Sicily and Naples, where only ten species of the fossils were extinct. The older Pliocene deposits, with one-third to one-half recent species, were those of the Sub-Apennines, and the English Crag. The deposits of the Loire, Bordeaux, Vienna, and others, containing about 18 per cent of recent species, he called Miocene, from μειων minor, and καινος recens—a minority only of recent species. The oldest of the tertiaries he termed Eocene, "from ηως aurora, and καινος recens, because the extremely small proportion of living species contained in these strata indicates what may be considered the first commencement or *dawn* of the existing state of the animate creation". To this epoch belonged the deposits of the London and Paris Basins, with only $3\frac{1}{2}$ per cent of living species. He fully recognized that, like any classification, it was arbitrary, "for the convenience of systematic arrangement", and thought the apparent distinctness due to lack of evidence of intermediate deposits. He himself later substituted the term Pleistocene for the late Pliocene.

The rest of the book was devoted to a graphic description of scenery representing every type of rock. He went into greatest detail for the tertiary deposits, reconstructing their possible manner of formation, and exploring volcanic, marine and fresh-water deposits for each era. In dealing with the secondary rocks he made one of his rare blunders, for he attributed the erosion of the chalk in the south of England to the sea. For him, the Downs were ancient sea-cliffs. All his life he was inclined to place too much emphasis on marine action, and too little on subaerial erosion, as Scrope pointed out in 1830.

The elucidation of the tertiary strata was probably Lyell's greatest contribution to factual geological knowledge. He continued, however, with his original researches for the rest of his life, jealously guarding his time and energy for the purpose, and refusing many other commitments. He did, after considerable hesitation, accept for a time the Chair of Mineralogy and Geology at King's College, London. He gave a series of highly successful lectures in the years 1832 and 1833—lectures at which ladies were present—a great, and apparently disrupting, innovation in Victorian scholastic circles. In later years, he accepted the presidency of the Geological Society, and he frequently presided over the geological section of the British Association. But he was always parsimonious of time spent in this way. His real love was to travel, and he spent no less than one-quarter of his active life in travel, often accompanied by his wife—for he married Mary Horner, daughter of another geologist, in 1832. In Norway and Sweden he verified the gradual rising of the land. In America, where he made two long visits based on lecture tours, he examined the great fossil forests of Nova Scotia, and estimated the rate of recession of the falls of Niagara. At the age of 61, he revisited Etna and slept for four nights in a shelter at 10,000 ft. It was on this occasion that he wrote "a good mule is like presenting an old geologist with a young pair of legs".

Two other contributions of special significance may perhaps be selected from a continual stream of publications and papers, often read first at the Geological Society. These are his work on glacial phenomena in Scotland, and his last work, the *Antiquity of Man*.

It was not until 1840 that it was dreamed that glaciation had occurred extensively in Scotland. In that year, Agassiz, the Swiss ichthyologist, came to the British Association meeting in Glasgow, at the invitation of Buckland. Agassiz had already been convinced of the former action of land ice in Switzerland. He immediately recognized glacial markings in the neighbourhood of Glasgow,

F

and much more extensive evidence in the Highlands. Three
papers were presented in London in November 1840, by Agassiz,
Buckland, and Lyell. These papers represent a first attempt to
deal with glaciation in the British Isles. They were received with
such incredulity that Lyell seems scarcely to have believed them
himself. It was not until 1857 that he was able to examine Swiss
glaciers in action, and compare their effects with the Scottish
remains. He found the parallels entirely convincing.

The *Antiquity of Man* was published in 1863, when Lyell was
65. As a young man, Lyell had believed that man was too recent
to have ever seen a living mammoth. In his life-time, however,
more and more flint tools of undoubted human workmanship
were being unearthed, in conjunction with fossil remains of
mammoths and other extinct animals. In 1826 Jacques Boucher de
Perthes had discovered worked flints in ancient gravel beds of the
Somme at Abbeville, and at about the same time similar discoveries were made at Kent's Hole near Torquay. Lyell, himself,
as early as 1833, had seen fossil bones and flint tools collected
from caves near Liège. In 1858, a virgin cave was discovered at
Brixham, near Torquay, which could be used as a test case. Its
investigation was entrusted to William Pengelly, who had
already explored Kent's Hole. His results were decisive. Under
an unbroken layer of stalagmite, sealing the floor of the cave,
flint implements and fossil bones were found together. Their
contemporaneity could no longer remain in doubt. In 1859
Pengelly conducted Lyell through the excavations. That same
year, as President of the Geological section of the British Association, Lyell placed these findings before the scientific world; laid
upon the table as he spoke were flint implements which he had
himself collected at Abbeville. This announcement marked
another milestone in man's understanding of the history of the
globe; his own origins were pushed back to pre-glacial times.

Lyell's *Antiquity of Man* was a survey of these and other findings
concerning human origins. Darwin somewhat uncharitably called
it a compilation, and this was true in that it collected together the
original work of other men. But it was a compilation verified

where possible by personal observation on the prehistoric sites. In the book, Lyell ranged widely over all the remains of early man then known, from those of Recent times, found in Danish peat bogs, to the famous Post-Pliocene skull found at Neanderthal, near Dusseldorf in 1856. He described fully the flint cultures found throughout Europe, especially those of the Somme Valley and of Southern England. Thus he reversed his long-held opinion on the recency of man.

So, Sir Charles Lyell came, full of years and honour, to the end of a successful and happy life, still intellectually supple enough to be open to new ideas. The following is a description of him in his last years, written by his secretary:

> Above the medium height and having a well-shaped head and clear-cut intellectual features (with a forehead of surprising height and width), Lyell would have been a man of commanding presence if his extremely short sight had not obliged him to stoop and to peer into anything he wished to observe. When dictating, he was often restless, moving from his chair to his sofa, pacing the room, or sometimes flinging himself full length on two chairs, tracing a pattern with his finger on the floor, as some thoughtful or eloquent passage flowed from his lips.

His reputation was unequalled perhaps in Europe in his own chosen field. His *magnum opus*, the *Principles of Geology*, ran to eleven editions in his lifetime, each one carefully brought up-to-date by Lyell. "To sketch the life and labours of Sir Charles Lyell would be much the same thing as sketching the development of the modern school of British geology during well-nigh half a century", ran the tribute in the *Academy* after his death in 1875, at the age of 77. The citation for the Copley Medal, awarded him in 1858, had hailed him as a leader in almost every branch of geology.

Leader perhaps describes him most accurately. Science moves forward in a number of ways; sometimes by the originality and genius of a Galileo; sometimes by the intuitive guesswork of a Pasteur; sometimes by the logic and dogged hard work of a Madame Curie. These work in isolation. Also vital to the story are the men who consolidate, and teach, and fill in the details. Lyell, for all his original researches, was essentially one of these;

a man in advance of his times, undoubtedly, but not so far in advance that he was unable to close the gap, and carry the times forward with him. His work had combatted old error effectively when, as a young man, he had stood alone. It had paved the way for new adventures of thought. More can hardly be expected of the work of any man.

SUGGESTIONS FOR FURTHER READING

Sir Charles Lyell, *Life, Letters and Journals*, 1881.
Sir Charles Lyell, *Principles of Geology*, First edition, 1830–3.
Edward Bailey, *Charles Lyell*, 1962.
Loren Eiseley, *Darwin's Century*, 1959.
Charles C. Gillispie, *Genesis and Geology*, 1959.
Gertrude Himmelfarb, *Darwin and the Darwinian Revolution*, 1959.

CHAPTER 6

ADOLPHE QUETELET, 1796–1874

> I should wish to reside in Bonn on the return of Spring and to pass my days on the borders of the Rhine. I would renounce all study, my mind only occupied with the animating scene which that fine river presents. I see here boats crossing in all directions, and travellers of all nations coming to pay their homage to one of the fairest and richest valleys in the world. These waves that flow so rapidly before me, whence come they? . . . I already calculate the velocity of the water and ask myself . . . What is its average rate?

So writes Lambert Adolphe Jacques Quetelet in introducing a discourse on means and averages.

This man of science and letters was born in Ghent on 22 February 1796. Few details of his childhood are on record. His father, a native of Picardie in Northern France, was evidently a man of some education, who at an early age ventured across the English Channel and became secretary to a Scottish nobleman. In this capacity he travelled extensively throughout Europe before settling in the ancient town of Ghent, to become some kind of municipal officer, rendering the town "valuable and well esteemed services". When he died in 1803, Adolphe was only seven, and it is likely that his mother encouraged the boy in the wide range of intellectual interests which he was soon to pursue.

Besides showing great mathematical ability, Adolphe Quetelet became dramatist and poet, artist and musician. In 1812 he attracted public attention with a drawing exhibited at Ghent, and which had been awarded first prize at the Lycée de Ghent. A more modest standard of attainment was reached in his playing of the flute. At twenty he wrote, along with a friend, the libretto for a one act opera which was successfully performed in Ghent, and this was followed by further dramas. Much of his poetry was published and was well received, while his natural interest in, and affection for, his fellow creatures was to bring him success as a teacher and friends from various classes of society.

Quetelet's teaching career began in Audenaerde in 1813 following his graduation at the Lyceum in his native town, and two years later, when still only nineteen, he became an instructor in mathematics at the Royal College in Ghent. In 1817 the University of Ghent was founded, and Quetelet became part teacher, part pupil, attending lectures in advanced mathematics by Jean Garnier, Professor of Astronomy and Mathematics. The influence of M. Garnier was decisive. Of him Quetelet later writes: "Little by little, his conversation, always instructive and animated, gave special direction to my tastes, which would have led me by preference towards letters."

So it was that the wheel came to rest pointing the young Quetelet in the direction of mathematics and the physical sciences. Success followed success. After becoming the first to receive the degree of Doctor of Science from the new University—with a work on the properties of conic sections—he was elected Professor of Elementary Mathematics in the Athenaeum at Brussels. The year was 1819. He was still only 23. Here he was to remain for the next nine years, during the last five of which he occupied the Chair of Higher Mathematics.

The biography of Quetelet is largely the study of an intellectual development, of expanding interests and the unfolding of new ideas. What then were the influences and achievements of this settled yet formative period of his life?

THE TEACHER AND THE MAN

Quetelet's first duty was clearly to teach, and this he did brilliantly. On students who showed any special aptitude he lavished great personal attention, taking pleasure in imparting his own knowledge and experience. He was "considerate and amiable, free from pedantry and conceit, and endowed with a

PLATE 15. Adolphe Quetelet.

true talent for exposition". A series of popular lectures given at the Museum attracted great attention from all classes of Society. In these he expounded the secrets of physics, astronomy, geometry, differential and integral calculus and probability. One of his most distinguished pupils, Joseph Plateau, said later, in dedicating to Quetelet his "Statique expérimentale",

> You, who have been one of the active promoters of the intellectual regeneration of Belgium, and whose works have so much contributed to the image of this country; you, who have guided my first steps in a scientific career, and who have taught me, by your example, to stimulate in the minds of the young a love for research; you, finally, who have never ceased to be for me a devoted friend . . .

The success of these lectures was such that in 1827 a "Musée des sciences et des lettres" was founded by Royal Decree on the basis of a plan drawn up by Quetelet. This institution provided a wide series of courses on philosophy, history, literature, mathematics, physics, chemistry, botany, zoology, etc. His own lectures included courses on the history of science. His election in 1820 to membership of the "Académie royale des sciences et belles lettres de Bruxelles", had already led to the writing of historical and biographical notes on many of his contemporaries. In all he produced more than fifty of these, covering such men as Ampère, Arago, Babbage, Cauchy, Goethe, Herschel, von Humboldt, and Malthus, and one surmises that his lectures must have stimulated scientist and layman alike.

Nor was his teaching confined to classroom or to after-dinner conversation with a pupil-friend. During this period at the Athenaeum there appeared the first volumes of *Correspondance mathématique et physique* with Quetelet and Garnier as joint editors. This became one of the leading journals in Europe with contributions from mathematicians and scientists in Britain, France, Germany, Holland and elsewhere. His interest in astronomy was growing, and of four popular works published between 1826 and 1828, two were *Astronomie élémentaire* and *Astronomie populaire*. Another was entitled *Positions de physique* while the fourth, *Instructions populaires sur le calcul des probabilités*, marked yet another subject to which Quetelet had become attracted, namely the study and methods of calculating probabilities. Some of these were later reprinted and translated into several foreign languages. Their simplicity of style and clarity of expression opened up new avenues of knowledge to the general reader. The second of the works on astronomy achieved the distinction of being placed on the Catholic Church's list of banned publications, a fact which is said to have further increased its popularity. *Positions de physique ou résumé d'un cours de physique générale* (to give it its full title) also merited high praise as "an extensive and succinct account of the different branches of physics".

Alongside this intense activity as a teacher, Quetelet, during his nine years at the Athenaeum, continued to enlarge the scope of his own knowledge. As early as 1820, the year of his appointment to the Chair of Elementary Mathematics, he had begun to arouse, among friends and colleagues, among learned societies and government ministers, interest in procuring an observatory. To acquire familiarity with the practical side of astronomy, he travelled to Paris in 1823, spending three months at the expense of the Belgian Government with the astronomers Arago and Bouvard. The latter introduced him to the methods and instruments used in observing the stars, as well as to a select inner circle of friends who were to have a profound effect on the mind of the young Belgian Professor. He met mathematicians and physicists, Laplace, Poisson, Fourier, von Humboldt and Fresnel. Fourier taught him mathematics, while from Laplace he learned more of the theory of probabilities, the concept of which from that time on affected his whole outlook.

On his return to Brussels events moved slowly in regard to the establishment of an observatory in the city, and it was not until 1827 that Quetelet was eventually "charged by the King with making the first purchase of instruments". Meanwhile he had married the daughter of a French physician and refugee, M. Curlet. She was a cultured woman and an accomplished musician with the result that their home became the meeting place of scientists, artists, and others. On Sunday evenings friends were invited to dinner which was often followed by music and charades.

His home life has been described as "of marked beauty and serenity", and he is said to have found great pleasure in his two children. The boy was later to become an able astronomer.

Nor had his love of the arts deserted him, and besides continuing to write poetry, he found time to translate in prose and verse romances from the literatures of England, Italy and Spain. He read French, Italian, Spanish, Portuguese, English, German and Dutch. Typical of this man of science was the publication in 1823 of his *Essai sur la romance*, a survey on romance of different peoples and the findings of the origin of romance in the days of chivalry.

THE ASTRONOMER

While Quetelet up until 1828 was mainly occupied in teaching, he yet remained active in his original field of research—geometry. In 1820 he published a synthesis of various earlier researches under the title *Nouvelle théorie des sections coniques considérées dans le solide*. After this he explored the field of caustic curves, publishing original work on this topic in a series of papers in the journals of the Académie and in *Correspondance mathématique et physique*, of which he was the sole editor until 1839.

However, notwithstanding the importance of these, Quetelet's ultimate claim to fame was in the field of applied research. From now on this aspect of his work comes under two distinct headings, and his achievements in either would have placed him among the leading scientists of his day. One of these arose from his interest in probability and is thought to represent his supreme contribution to scientific thought, but first we shall look briefly at the other.

Here we see Quetelet the astronomer.

In 1828 he left the Chair of Higher Mathematics in the Athenaeum to become astronomer of the Royal Observatory. Because of difficulties in obtaining financial support he was unable to take up the new appointment until 1832, and in the meantime spent much time travelling, accompanied by his wife. In Germany, Holland, Italy, Switzerland and France he visited astronomers and made numerous observations on the strength of terrestrial magnetic currents. They met Goethe on his eightieth birthday and spent eight happy days with the poet, discussing among other things the latter's optical theories. Earlier Quetelet had spent two months with his friend, Dandelin, in England, Scotland and Ireland, visiting universities, observatories and learned societies.

On returning to the Observatory, Quetelet instigated a wide range of research projects on astronomy, meteorology and physics of the globe. These included observations on meteors made simultaneously from four Belgian cities, on sunspot activity, on tides along the Belgian coast. Small telescopes were erected in another five cities, and sun-dials placed in forty-one towns. The longitude of Brussels relative to Greenwich was measured. Always he emphasized the importance of simultaneous observations at different points on the Earth's surface.

Quetelet's meteorological studies aroused interest throughout Europe. Following a suggestion of Fourier's he measured terrestrial temperatures. A study of atmospheric electricity resulted in the establishment of a relationship between intensity and height, on which discovery Wheatstone and Faraday wrote special reports to the British Association and the Royal Society respectively. At Herschel's suggestion, hourly meteorological observations at the time of the solstices and equinoxes were begun. Later, these were extended to every two hours throughout the year. Similar regular magnetic observations were carried out at the request of the Royal Astronomical Society of London.

Of the greatest importance to the future of weather forecasting and the understanding of atmospheric phenomena were Quetelet's hourly readings of barometric pressures made with the co-operation of observers throughout Europe. This led to the discovery of atmospheric waves whose form and velocity could be examined. Quetelet, responding to a request from Maury of Washington, called together at Brussels in 1853 a Sea Conference over which he himself presided. In an era so much less internationally minded than our own and with no highly developed systems of communication, one can imagine the effort of organization needed to bring together scientists in this way. The eminent success of the Conference was largely due to Quetelet's personal influence, his conviction and determination.

Similar co-operation from other scientists was sought and obtained in Quetelet's studies on the annual and diurnal habits of plants. Periodic phenomena intrigued him. Observations were made on times of blossoming, foliation, and of leaf fall. The driving force behind these far-ranging series of observations was the desire to establish laws of nature governing apparently unrelated events, to find regularity in seeming disorder. Apart from the use he himself made of these collections of data, their mere publication was a permanent legacy to the scientific world. In the opening paragraph of one of his letters, Quetelet writes:

> The habit of observing has not with me blunted the sentiment of admiration which I have ever felt at the sight of the heavens. The magnificence and the imposing regularity of this spectacle contrast marvellously, in the calm of the night, with the rapid and tumultuous succession of objects with which we have been occupied during the day—one feels, so to speak, transported into another world. The silence of an observatory, the monotonous and regular beat of the pendulum, and still more regular progress of the stars, add much to this illusion. We then better understand the weakness of man, and the power of the Supreme: we are struck with the inflexible constancy of the laws which regulate the march of worlds, and which preside over the succession of human generations.

WHAT IS STATISTICS?

Quetelet's interest in statistics developed alongside his interest in astronomy during his years at the Athenaeum. But first, what is understood by statistics today and what did it mean to Quetelet and his contemporaries?

Generally, any coherent set of figures, measurements or numerical classifications may be referred to as "statistics", and the study or manipulation of these has come to be known as the science of statistics. The statistician's field of activity is therefore a wide one.

Examples of one type of statistical problem arise from the collection of factual information on such topics as births and deaths, disease incidence, road accident rates, crime statistics, national import and export figures, cost of living fluctuations, distributions of incomes, meteorological measurements, farming practices, and so forth. The data having been collected (preferably in the way that he has suggested), the statistician may then be required to calculate various averages relating, say, to different regions or different years, and present these in tables from which the reader can make comparisons.

Here the statistician's job may end, it being left to the reader to interpret the data in his own way, by noting, for example, that over the last ten years there has been an increase in the number of serious crimes detected in the United Kingdom, whereas a trend in the opposite direction has been observed in Ruritania. On the other hand, the statistician may be required to investigate these and other possible trends or relationships in more detail, and this will require more elaborate statistical techniques than merely calculating totals or averages.

As well as the interpreter of numerical results, however, the statistician's role is equally that of adviser in the method of collection of the data and computer who calculates such estimates or summaries as are required. However, this is not a statistical text book, and we need not go into details of the methods of sampling and of estimation that are part of a statistician's equipment.

The reader may notice that the examples given earlier of various sort of data have all one thing in common. Whether they are social, economic, or naturally occurring such as meteorological data, they are all data over which the investigator is most unlikely to have any control. He certainly cannot vary the temperature of the Greenland ice-cap in order to study the effect on the winter rainfall of Leningrad. Nor is he likely to have more than a slender influence in parliamentary decisions to abolish or reintroduce the death penalty—if he had he might obtain useful comparisons of the numbers of murders committed in years in which the murderer can be hanged with those in which he cannot. These can all be grouped under the heading of "uncontrolled" data.

In contrast with "uncontrolled data" are "controlled" data arising out of deliberately planned experiments. In these, different experimental units are selected (usually in some objective, random manner) for allocation to the different conditions or "treatments" which the experimenter wishes to compare. This branch of statistics has made spectacular advances in more recent times, and the controlled experiment now occupies an important role in agriculture and biology, in medical, educational and psychological research, in the study of natural populations and in many aspects of industrial research. Since the need for statistics arises essentially from the variation in behaviour from one individual or experimental unit to another, its need is generally less felt in the exact sciences. Even so, in statistical physics we now find the same principles applied to the movement of particles in thermodynamics and nuclear physics, and to the continuous variation of an electro-magnetic field.

The difference between controlled and uncontrolled data is far-reaching when it comes to interpretation of results. With controlled data, if the difference between differently treated units is greater than can be attributed to chance, then this difference is due to the factor (treatment, variety, etc.) under test. With uncontrolled data, on the other hand, a similar difference might be associated with one or more factors, it being impossible to deduce which, if any, of these factors is the *cause*. For this reason uncontrolled data are notoriously difficult to interpret.

So far we have discussed, very sketchily, the application of statistics to a range of practical problems. To perform his duties effectively, the statistician requires to make use of numerous techniques of varying computational complexity, to estimate treatment effects, to test the statistical significance of observed differences, to measure degrees of association among variables or the form of this association, to develop new experimental designs and appropriate methods of analysis, to compare variabilities, and so forth. Underlying these techniques is a network of mathematical and statistical theory, and much of his time, or that of his more theoretically minded colleagues, must be devoted to research into new theoretical developments.

STATISTICS IN THE EARLY NINETEENTH CENTURY

In 1825, which marked the beginning of Quetelet's interest in statistics, the subject was in its infancy and bore little relation to statistics as we now understand it.

From the sixteenth century onwards studies had been made of nations and their resources. These were mainly descriptive in character and covered the geography, history, customs, industry, trade, political and ecclesiastical organization and military power of each country. The potential of a nation in terms of fighting men and war materials was of obvious political value to heads of states, and these surveys gradually developed in the extent to which they attempted to find causes for the observed phenomena. Thus were formed the beginnings of political theory.

By the second half of the eighteenth century two distinct schools of thought had emerged typified by Achenwall on the one hand and by Derham and Süssmilch on the other. Achenwall and his associates were primarily concerned with describing those aspects of a nation which would be of most value to statesmen and relied largely on verbal description. The other school concentrated its attention more on the study of social life, and used observation and enumeration as the foundation of its work. It acquired the title "School of political arithmetic", and performed calculations on numerical data from which conclusions and causes might be deduced.

The two schools eventually merged, and from then unified progress was made in the methods of procuring data and interpreting results. However, another branch of intellectual activity was now also gaining momentum. For its origin we turn to the gambling dens of the Middle Ages.

Gambling had long been established as a fashionable pastime with Frenchmen when, in 1654, the nobleman and gambler,

Chevalier de Méré, posed to the eminent mathematician, Pascal, certain problems on dice, in particular concerning the division of stakes among players who stopped before the end of their game. Pascal started a correspondence on the subject with his colleague, Fermat, and this marked the first attempt to treat probability seriously as a branch of mathematics.

Three years later the Dutch physicist, Huygens, followed with a treatise on the mathematical treatment of the chances of winning certain card and dice games, and this in turn led to the proposing and solving of further problems in probability by Jacques Bernoulli, Montmort, de Moivre and others. Bernoulli, a Swiss mathematician, by his *Ars Conjectandi*, published posthumously in 1713, became the author of the first book devoted wholly to the theory of probability.

Thus, from the gaming tables of the seventeenth century originated a third factor, the concept of probability, which was soon to provide the two schools of descriptive statistics with the mathematical robustness needed to put them on a scientific footing. At the same time probability continued to develop as an independent subject of study among pure mathematicians. Following further developments by Montmort and de Moivre during the next two or three decades, however, came a period of semi-dormancy, and it was not until near the close of the eighteenth century that Laplace awakened fresh interest in probability among mathematicians. From then until 1850 the subject moved rapidly ahead with a series of discoveries by Gauss and Bessel in Germany, Laplace, Poisson, Cauchy and Bravais in France, De Morgan in England, Adrain in America and Tchebycheff in Russia.

QUETELET THE STATISTICIAN

When Quetelet arrived on the scene, the stage was nicely set for one such as he to begin applying statistical methods on a wide scale. Gifted mathematician as he was, he made no attempt to research into probability theory as such. Rather did he see in the work of his friends, Laplace, Poisson and Fourier the great potential of their new-found techniques in other fields of study.

Quetelet's first statistical memoir appeared in 1825. In this he presented tables of births and deaths in Brussels with the aim of providing a reliable basis for life insurance. Later publications extended the mortality and population tables to cover the whole of Belgium. Distinctions were made between the sexes and whether residing in city or country, and mortality rates were examined for different ages of individual.

In the following year he became correspondent for the Statistical Bureau which had just been created in Holland, and immediately urged that a census be taken in that country. This was duly done in 1829 and three years later he was given charge of a similar census in Belgium. In 1841 he was largely responsible for the establishment of a Commission Centrale de Statistique and became its president, a post which he retained for the rest of his life.

He was particularly emphatic about the need for greater exactitude in the collecting of census data and did much to improve the standard of census-taking. To a more statistically minded generation his four guiding principles seem now to smack of the obvious, but we owe it to him and his successors that these have become accepted as essential in any survey. He exhorts the surveyor to

(1) Only obtain such information as is absolutely necessary, and such as you are sure to obtain.

(2) Avoid demands which may excite distrust and wound local interests or personal susceptibility, as well as those whose utility would not be sufficiently appreciated.

(3) Be precise and clear, in order that the enquiries may be everywhere understood in the same manner, and that the answers may be comparable. Adopt for this purpose uniform schedules which may be filled up uniformly.

(4) Collect the documents in such a way that verification may be possible.

His position gave him access to much official data, and there followed other publications on populations statistics—on the Belgian prisons and lodging houses for the poor, illegitimate births and the courts of law. The moral aspect of his work often impressed Quetelet, as when he notes the effect of a vicious administration on the health of the men in the prison at Vilvorde. Here "there reigned, during the years 1802, 1803 and 1804, such a mortality that never men during the most frightful plagues, never were soldiers during the most frightful wars, decimated in a more frightful manner. Annually three prisoners out of every four died". In contrast he found that "in the house of correction at Ghent the deaths were proportionately less numerous than in the privileged classes of Society".

The statistics of crime formed one of his main subjects for enquiry. In *Recherches sur le penchant au crime aux différents âges* he breaks down detected crimes to show the effect of educational level, climate, sex and age on the propensity to commit crimes. Crimes against people are distinguished from crimes against property. As in all such studies, his aim was continually to look for causes. Mere collection and presentation of data was of no real value unless it were accompanied by some purpose. The proportions of individuals comprising these different categories were to him a means of measuring something more fundamental. Since crimes, for example, tend to reflect the social condition of the community, comparisons of conditions with respect to different times or places could be made by appropriate comparisons among the observations.

A fact which particularly impressed Quetelet and to which he made frequent reference was the constancy of the number of crimes committed from year to year. He reflects,

> Thus we pass from one year to another with the sad perspective of seeing the same crimes reproduced in the same order and calling down the same punishments in the same proportions. Sad condition of humanity! The part of prisons, of irons and of the scaffold seems fixed for it as much as the revenue of the state. We might enumerate in advance how many individuals will stain their hands in the blood of their fellows, how many will be forgers, how many will be poisoners, almost as we can enumerate in advance the deaths and births that should occur.

Herein was a law—a social law—comparable to a law in physics. By affording a scientific rather than a theological interpretation to these facts, he threw doubt on man's free will. Given a particular social condition there was a certain probability that a crime would be committed in a given interval of time. As a result, the number of crimes expected in a given year was determined, and the observed number would not differ greatly from this hypothetical value. These conceptions, though not new, were stated so frequently and with such persuasion by Quetelet that the study of social conditions was soon elevated to the level of a scientific discipline.

In 1833 Quetelet attended the British Association meeting in Cambridge as the official Belgian delegate, as a result of which a statistical section was immediately founded with Babbage as chairman and Quetelet as one of its members. Considering the scope of this section too narrowly limited by the rules of the Association "he accordingly suggested to M. Babbage, from whom we have the statement, the formation of a statistical society in London." This society was founded in the following year, later becoming the Royal Statistical Society, and now one of the leading societies of its kind. In the same year Quetelet was elected a corresponding member of the British Association.

INTERNATIONAL STATISTICS

More and more of Quetelet's time and thoughts were now directed towards statistics. Nevertheless, he remained active in the work of the Observatory until 1857 when most of his duties were taken over by his son, who succeeded his father as director. His other main interest was the work of the Brussels Academy, in whose activities he participated to the end of his life.

We have already referred to his successful efforts to have regular meteorological observations taken simultaneously in different parts of Europe, but his vision extended beyond this. In his *Sur la physique du globe* and *Météorologie de la Belgique comparée à celle du globe* he conceives the possibility of a global physics based on world wide observations of the magnetic, meteorological, animal and vegetable phenomena of the earth with a view to discovering some pattern in the measurements.

An example of the kind of investigation to which he thus led is afforded by his study of time of blossoming of the lilac. His own description, taken from Downe's translation of Quetelet's *Lettres sur la théorie des probabilites*, embodies many of his principles and is worth quoting in part.

He begins by noting the variation in date of flowering of the lilac in Brussels over several consecutive years, and goes on to consider possible causes for such variation. He decides that "these causes can only be deduced from meteorological circumstances", and continues,

> Among meteorological influences, it is agreed to place in the first rank that of the temperature. It is thus that observers have first directed their attention to the study of this cause. Réaumur, I believe, first thought of taking the sum of temperatures, with a view to ascertain the day on which a vegetable phenomenon should occur. The Abbé Cotte followed this idea; and in his opinion the opening of a flower was the result of the temperatures to which the plant had been previously subject. In other respects, the date which served him for a starting point was quite artificial; he reckoned from 1 April. It is sufficient to transport ourselves in thought to the southern hemisphere, in order to see how small a real value this epoch has. Another equally well founded objection may be made to this mode of reckoning—it is that all the degrees of the thermometer have the same value, whether they refer to hot or cold days. Three days of a temperature of 8° centigrade (46° Fahrenheit) in the month of June, for example, should produce the same effect as one day at 24° centigrade (108° Fahrenheit). But these three cold days, following one another at the time when the sap is in all its activity, will rather retard vegetation; whilst a temperature of 24° (centigrade) will give it a new force, and will cause a great number of flowers to open.

After proposing a more logical method of fixing the starting point, by the date of cessation of the winter frosts, he then puts forward a modified hypothesis.

> I have already stated what leads me to regard as faulty the proceeding by which Cotte and the botanists who have followed him calculate the epochs of blossoming. The force exercised by the temperature is of the same nature as actual force. It is by the sum of the squares of the degrees, and not by the simple sum of the degrees, that we must appreciate its action. To put my conjecture to a trial, I have formed two tables, for each of the years of observation—the one containing the sum of temperatures, and the other the sum of the squares of the same temperatures from the fixed period which has been previously discussed. I have found, on comparing

these two tables, that on average 462° (centigrade) of temperature are required to produce the flowering of the lilac according to the ideas of Cotte, and a total of 4,264, as the sum of the squares of the several degrees, according to my method of reckoning.

Admitting these numbers, and seeking the dates to which they correspond in my two tables, calculated as I have just stated, I find as the epoch of flowering:—

| EPOCHS | ACCORDING TO | | ACCORDING TO OBSERVATION |
	Temperature	Squares of the temperature	
1839	10·5 May	9·3 May	10 May
1840	4·0 May	2·2 May	28 April
1841	23·5 April	23·0 April	24 April
1842	22·5 April	27·3 April	28 April
1843	19·5 April	19·7 April	20 April
1844	22·0 April	23·5 April	25 April
MEAN . . .	27·0 April	27·5 April	27·5 April

These numbers only agree with the numbers observed so far as to leave the question undecided. However, the method I propose gives more satisfactory values, especially for the year 1842. As one single plant could not resolve the difficulty, my observations have necessarily been extended to a great number of plants; and I think that the total results can leave no doubt.

The greatest variations, calculating by the second method, are generally within the limits of probable error.

Admitting the number 4,264 as that which corresponds to the epoch of the flowering of the lilac, we may by subtracting the squares of the temperatures of each preceding day arrive at the epoch of revival.

If plants, in order to blossom, were only subject to the action of the temperature, we should attach to each a number analogous to 4,264, which would determine the instant of its flowering, whether in a green-house or in any region whatever of the globe. This would be a *constant cause.*

Let us suppose that we have in fact determined the mode of action of the temperature, and that we could reckon its influence, we should know what correction each of the dates above enumerated should undergo. But if the temperature were the sole influencing cause, after the correction was made, the dates should become identically the same, or at least should only differ within the limits which relate to the uncertainties of observation. Admitting that they were actually within these limits, it would become very difficult, without a great number of observations, to determine the actions of other influencing causes, since these actions would lose themselves in the effects of accidental causes.

If, on the contrary, after having submitted the dates to the corrections required for temperature, we yet find differences which cannot be justified by the errors of the observations, we must seek to explain them by the influence of winds, the quantity of rain, the state of the heavens, or other meteorological causes. But in making use of the observations that I have been able to collect, I find that the correction for the temperature alone is sufficient to bring the calculated period of flowering within limits which include the uncertainties of observation: it will be useless then at present to seek to proceed further.

Here, by likening temperature to a mechanical force he formulates the hypothesis that the time of flowering depends not on the direct cumulative sum of daily temperatures but rather on the sums of their squares. Quetelet is proceeding in a reasonable scientific manner by testing his hypothesis on the data available. He then argues, with some justification, that the new hypothesis provides more reliable forecasts for date of flowering than did the old.

The twentieth-century biologist might well criticize these hypotheses and, in particular, would probably wish to take account of day-length as well as temperature. However, it is with Quetelet's statistical method that we are primarily concerned here.

The references to *constant* and *accidental* causes are repeated time and again throughout his statistical writings. They also constitute one of the fundamental principles of modern statistical thinking. When translated into current terminology what he is saying is that the observed time to flowering in a particular locality may be regarded as the sum of two parts, the first measuring the effect of temperature (his constant cause), and the second due to chance effects (his accidental causes) which may be either positive or negative, sometimes increasing and sometimes decreasing the observed value from what it would otherwise be. A chance effect, or "error" as it is now called, might be, as he suggests, the influence of winds. However, if in comparing flowering dates of two localities, one locality was *consistently* more exposed to winds than another, then the effect of wind would to a large extent become part of the effect associated with locality, that is, part of the "constant cause".

Quetelet next proceeds to compare dates of flowering for several different places. He continues:

> Drawing from these different sources, I have succeeded in forming the following table, in which will be found the epochs of the flowering of the lilac in the different years, and also the *mean epochs* calculated in comparison with the observations at Brussels.
>
> The mean epochs are calculated in the following manner. The lilac flowered at Parma in 1843 on the 10th April, that is ten days earlier than at Brussels; in 1844 it flowered eight days earlier than at Brussels: so that the mean advance was nine days for these two single observations. But the lilac blossoms at Brussels on the 28th April: we may therefore conclude that the date of flowering in Parma is the 19th April.
>
> These observations are still too few for the results to be accepted with confidence: many dates are only determined from one year's observation. We should have patience to collect the notes of many consecutive years, so as to eliminate from the general results everything accidental in the particular determinations.

Then follows the table.

EPOCH OF THE BLOSSOMING OF THE LILAC

PLACE OF OBSERVATION	1839	1840	1841	1842	1843	1844	MEAN EPOCH
Parma	..	..	..	..	10 April	17 April	19 April
Venice	..	..	..	..	..	16 April	19 April
Paris	..	..	..	20 April	..	..	21 April
Brussels	10 May	28 April	24 April	28 April	20 April	25 April	28 April
Liege	..	..	25 April	..	..	..	29 April
Louvain	..	..	29 April	27 April	..	..	30 April
Ghent	..	..	28 April	30 April	23 April	27 April	1 May
Bruges	..	..	..	..	26 April	..	4 May
Ostend	..	..	..	10 May	26 April	..	7 May
Utrecht	..	..	..	6 May	..	6 May	7 May
Joppa, Deventer	..	..	..	..	..	5 May	8 May
Lochem, Gueldre	..	..	..	..	..	7 May	10 May
Groningen Friesland	..	..	..	12 May	..	..	12 May
Prague	..	8 May	8 May	8 May	3 May	..	10 May
Environs of Cambridge	..	..	..	..	1 May	..	9 May
Munich	..	..	..	2 May	6 May	4 May	10 May
State of New York	16 May	16 May	26 May	16 May	22 May	..	21 May

Quetelet's method of calculating his mean epochs is to average not the actual dates but the *differences* between these dates and the corresponding dates for Brussels. This prevents the means from being biased in the sense that if 1843 and 1844, for example, had chanced to be two unusually "early" years, the straight average of the two Parma dates would give an earlier mean epoch than would the similar calculation from all six years. Even though a more elaborate and more efficient method of adjusting for this bias would be used today, Quetelet's procedure is an eminently successful attempt to improve the reliability of statistical estimates.

Implied in his calculation of the mean epochs is the assumption that the constant causes act in such a way that any particular locality tends to be always the same number of days different from Brussels, and any variation in the observed differences is due entirely to accidental causes. Thus, the differences between Parma and Brussels of 10 and 8 days are acceptable as unbiased estimates for the differences that would have been obtained in the other four years, and this justifies acceptance of their mean of 9 days as the appropriate amount to subtract from 28 April to get the mean epoch for Parma. However, it is conceivable that 1843 and 1844 might have had a weather pattern that favoured Parma more than it did Brussels, whereas in the remaining four years the reverse may have been true. If this were so the 19 April would be unduly early as an estimate of the mean epoch. Thus, the mean epochs so calculated would depend on for which years data was available. This point is not discussed by Quetelet, although he does emphasize the need to collect observations from "many consecutive years" so as to reduce the prominence of accidental causes.

USE OF THE NORMAL DISTRIBUTION

Another dominant theme of Quetelet's writings was his concept of "the average man". He regarded a nation as represented by "a type-man, a man who represents his people as to height (or other attribute) and in relation to whom all the other men of the same nation might be considered as presenting variations more or less great". Comparisons could therefore be made between nations or between any other groups of men by measuring large numbers of each and finding their averages.

Over a century earlier, about 1721, De Moivre, starting, in effect, with the binomial expansion of $(\frac{1}{2} + \frac{1}{2})^n$ and then letting n tend to infinity, had found that in the limit the $(r + 1)$th term became equal to

$$\frac{1}{\sqrt{2\pi}} e^{-\frac{x^2}{2}}$$

where x equalled $\dfrac{r - \frac{1}{2}n}{\sqrt{n}}$ and could take any value from $-\infty$ to $+\infty$.

Just as the $(r + 1)$th term in the binomial expansion was known to give the probability of obtaining r heads in n tosses of an unbiased coin, so did the above expression, when integrated over a range of x, give the probability of obtaining values of x within this range. The distribution thus defined was known to mathematicians as the "normal distribution" or the "normal law of errors".

During the first three decades of the nineteenth century the normal law of errors had come into general use by astronomers and physicists, and had been used in problems relating to artillery fire. The first serious attempt to apply it to social matters, however, was made by Quetelet. He assumed that measurements of individuals distributed themselves about that of the average man according to the normal law of errors. An examination of the chest measurement of 5738 Scottish soldiers gave good agreement with the normal curve. So also did the heights of 100,000 French conscripts, except that he noticed a congestion below the required height and a scarcity just above it, indicating "that some 2000 have escaped service by reducing their height two or three centimetres". These ideas were expanded in 1835 under the title, *Sur l'homme et le développement de ses facultés ou essai de physique sociale.*

Quetelet then generalized the concept to include not only physical measurements but also intellectual and moral qualities. His talent for clear and detailed explanation led him to publish in 1848 a three-volume work on the subject entitled *Du système social et des lois qui le régissent*. Quetelet in fact became greatly devoted to his "average man", whom he regarded as typifying perfection in beauty and goodness. Nature was construed as always "striving to produce the type", and failing only because of the interference of accidental causes which produced variation about the ideal.

A critic might be forgiven for maintaining that he overstated his case and often wandered into superfluous and fruitless discussion which added little to the knowledge of mankind. Such criticism, however, misses the point that the importance of Quetelet's work lay not in its immediate contribution to knowledge but in his method of acquiring it. His studies on the physical qualities of men led to the physical measurements of criminals being used as a means of identification, and provided anthropologists with the tools needed for racial differentiation. The basis was laid for a science of psychology, of education and of social life, while a new subject, biometry—the study through measurement, of living material—was beginning to take shape.

An illustration of his use of the normal distribution is given in another of his *Letters on Probabilities* in regard to measurements of the position of the Pole Star. Instead of calculating probabilities from the normal exponential curve quoted above, Quetelet seemed to prefer to use his own "scale of possibility" derived from the various proportions of black and white balls expected in a sample of 999 balls drawn from an infinite population in which black and white are mixed together in equal proportions. With a number as large as 999, the binomial probabilities so derived will, of course, be extremely close to those of the normal distribution. Thus, the probability of obtaining any specified number of white balls in the sample is given by the height of the corresponding pillar in the following diagram from his letter.

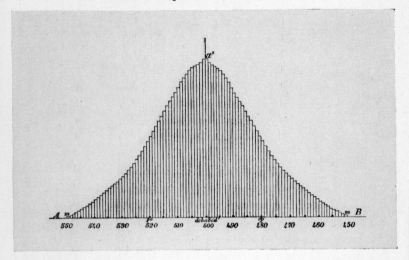

The probability of getting more than 550 or less than 450 balls is clearly very small. The normal curve is the smooth curve that would be obtained if the number 999 was increased indefinitely, and the horizontal distances telescoped correspondingly so as to keep the diagram within the width of the page. Quetelet writes:

I believe it is superfluous to mention that, in the example with which we are about to be occupied, I continue to admit that the chances of making errors in excess are exactly the same as those of making them in defect. The observations which I shall use are taken from the publications of the Royal Observatory at Greenwich: they refer to the determinations in time of the right ascension of the Polar Star; and by these words "right ascension" must be understood the distance of a star from the equinoctial point, measured along the celestial equator. I have employed for this purpose the observations of the Polar Star, obtained during the four years 1836 to 1839 inclusive. These observations have been corrected for nutation, precession, etc., and have been calculated for one particular time; so that they may not differ from one another, but by the effect of small accidental errors.

The first column of the following table indicates how much the observations differ from the mean in excess or defect. In order to be able to group the observations, I have marked $0^s \cdot 5$ for the difference in right ascension where the variations from the mean were included between the limits $0^s \cdot 25$ and $0^s \cdot 75$. In the same manner, the differences which fall between $0^s \cdot 75$ and $1^s \cdot 25$ have been united as forming variations of one second; and so on. As to the observations which do not differ $0^s \cdot 25$ from the mean more or less, they are considered as equal to the mean.

Differences in right ascension with regard to the mean	Number of observations in each group	
	by calculation	by experience
$-3^s \cdot 5$	4	2
$-3 \cdot 0$	10	12
$-2 \cdot 5$	22	25
$-2 \cdot 0$	46	43
$-1 \cdot 5$	82	74
$-1 \cdot 0$	121	126
$-0 \cdot 5$	152	150
Mean	163	168
$+0 \cdot 5$	147	148
$+1 \cdot 0$	112	129
$+1 \cdot 5$	72	78
$+2 \cdot 0$	40	33
$+2 \cdot 5$	19	10
$+3 \cdot 0$	10	2
	1000	1000

Quetelet then sets out to compare the observed numbers in the various groups with the theoretical numbers obtained from his own scale of possibility, after suitable adjustment of the two horizontal scales of measurement. His explanation is somewhat lengthy and involves the use of two tables. We need, therefore, only reproduce the resulting figures in the second column of the above table, these being the numbers expected on average if the measurements were, in fact, normally distributed.

The total number of observations was actually 487, but he has chosen to multiply the numbers observed in each grouping interval by $\dfrac{1000}{487}$ to simulate the distribution that would have been obtained from 1000 observations. (In general this last step is reprehensible, but for his present purpose it makes little difference.) These numbers appear in the final column of the table.

Quetelet concludes that the numbers arrived at by calculation

> differ very little from those which experience has in reality furnished. It would be difficult for calculation and experiment to agree better. This agreement is a proof of the skill of the English observers.
>
> I wish to be allowed to make one further remark. We have just seen that a difference of $0^s \cdot 5$ in the right ascension of the Polar Star corresponds in the table of precision to six ranks and a half: proportionately, twenty-one ranks constitute the probable error: there is then 1 to bet against 1 that the variations from the mean do not pass the half of $1^s \cdot 61$ or $0^s \cdot 8$. The *probable error* is then here eight-tenths of a second in time.

The probable error is, by definition, the distance from the mean in each direction within which half the observations lie. Thus, for a given distribution, the probable error measures the scatter about the mean. It has since been superseded by a similar measure called the standard error, the probable error for the normal distribution being $0 \cdot 67449$ times the standard error.

In other words, the main conclusion is that the errors of measurement of the "right ascension" of the Pole Star follow a normal distribution with a probable error of $0 \cdot 8$ seconds. Certain remarks invite comment.

Quetelet offers no real justification for his belief that "the chances of making errors in excess are exactly the same as those of making them in defect". Even if the distribution were, as he assumes, symmetrical about the mean, it is still quite possible for a consistent error in one direction to cause each measurement to be a fixed amount higher, say, than it would otherwise be. A bias of this kind is very common and often very troublesome. Only by comparison with the results from some other, supposedly better, method of observation can it be detected.

Nor would it be unusual to find some asymmetry in measurements of this kind. Quetelet was well aware of asymmetry in other situations, such as in daily temperature and barometrical readings, in price fluctuations and mortality counts. In regard to repeated measurements of the same thing, however, he not only expected symmetry, but regarded agreement with normality as evidence of skilful observation. While admitting that there is some measure of truth in this belief, one can hardly approve his statement that "this agreement is proof of the skill of the English observers". A more suitable criterion of skill would be the size of the probable error.

Quetelet might well have gone a step further by noting that whereas $0 \cdot 8$ is the probable error of any one observation from the set, the mean of 487 observations would have had a probable error of only $0 \cdot 8 \sqrt{487}$, that is, $0 \cdot 073$. This would have illustrated his oft-repeated maxim that conclusions should never be based on a few observations but only on the average of a large number.

THE CLOSING YEARS

In the summer of 1855, at the age of 59, Quetelet suffered a stroke while studying on the veranda of his home. Though recovering in a few weeks, his mind never quite regained its previous alertness, and his writing became tedious and repetitious, needing thorough revision. The death of his wife and daughter came as a heavy blow. Yet he continued his work at the Academy and the Observatory, and his pen was never long at rest. Two major historical works were even produced, *Sciences mathématiques et physiques chez les Belges* (1864 and 1866), and he lived long enough to see, in 1873, the First International Meteorological Congress which was a sequel to the Sea Conference over which he had presided twenty years earlier. On this occasion he was represented by his son, and his plan for co-ordinated observations on natural phenomena was the central theme of discussion.

On 17 February 1874, Quetelet, after a brief illness, died. Hankins writes: "His funeral was the occasion of a most numerous and distinguished gathering of members of royal families, scientists, men of letters and representatives of learned societies (he was a member of more than a hundred). Funds for a statue of him were soon raised by popular subscription, the monument being unveiled in Brussels in 1880."

Two final quotations aptly summarize his life. The first is again from Hankins:

> Quetelet's personality is represented as most winning. Modest and generous, convinced but respectful of others' opinions, calm and considerate, a man of broad learning and an attractive conversationalist, he won and kept friends wherever he went. A man of excellent tact, as well as of tremendous enthusiasm, he readily enlisted support for many schemes of co-operative scientific endeavour. A man of wide intellectual interests, and at the same time endowed with a prodigious capacity for labour, he contributed to the advancement of several sciences, aroused anew the entire intellectual life of his country and stimulated the activity of artists and scientists throughout the world. Until the attack of 1855, he is represented as always animated and genial, fond of wit and laughter. 'Rabelais was almost as dear to him as Pascal'.

The second quotation is Quetelet's introduction to the course he gave on the history of science at the "Musée des sciences et des lettres". He was then a young professor, but his statement will doubtless stand the test of time, and is a fitting epitaph on his own life's work.

> The more advanced the sciences have become, the more they have tended to enter the domain of mathematics, which is a sort of centre towards which they converge. We can judge of the perfection to which a science has come by the facility, more or less great, with which it may be approached by calculation.

REFERENCES AND FURTHER READING

FITZPATRICK, P. J. Leading British statisticians of the nineteenth century. *Journal of the American Statistical Association* **55**, 1960, 38–70.

HANKINS, F. H. *Adolphe Quetelet as a Statistician.* New York, Faculty of Political Science of Columbia University (*Studies in History, Economics and Public Law*), 1908.

MAILLY, E. *Essai sur vie et les oeuvres de L. A. J. Quetelet.* Bruxelles, Hayez, 1875.

QUETELET, A. *Lettres à S.A.R. le duc régnant de Saxe-Cobourg et Gotha, sur la théorie des probabilités, appliquée aux sciences morales et politiques.* Bruxelles, Hayez, 1846.

QUETELET, A. *Letters addressed to H.R.H. the Grand Duke of Saxe-Cobourg and Gotha, on the theory of probabilités as appliéd to the moral and political sciences* (translated by O. G. Downes). London, Charles and Edwin Layton, 1849.

WALKER, H. M. *Studies in the History of Statistical Method, with special reference to certain educational problems.* Baltimore, Williams and Wilkins, 1931.

WEAVER, W. *Lady Luck, The Theory of Probability.* London, Heinemann, 1964.